Causes Behind the Increase and Decrease of *Eemaan*

by Shaykh 'Abdur-Razzaaq al-'Abbaad

Translated by Abu Safwan Farid ibn Abdulwahid Haibatan

ISBN 1 898649 37 5

British Library Cataloguing in Publication Data.
A catalogue record for this book is available from the British Library.

First Edition, 1420 AH/1999 CE

Typeset by: Al-Hidaayah Publishing and Distribution

Published by: Al-Hidaayah Publishing and Distribution
P.O. Box 3332
Birmingham
United Kingdom
B10 9AW

Tel: 0121 753 1889
Fax: 0121 753 2422
E-Mail: sales@al-hidaayah.co.uk
Internet: www.al-hidaayah.co.uk

Printed by: Alltrade Printers (Sales) Ltd, Birmingham, U.K.

Contents

Translator's Note

All praise is for Allaah, Lord of the worlds and may He praise, send peace and blessings upon our Messenger, his family and Companions.

The greatest blessing Allaah, the Most High, can bestow upon a person in this world is the blessing of *eemaan*. It is as the author points out in his introduction the source to all the good in this world and Hereafter. However, as the texts unequivocally show and as a simple glance at the various types of people will show, *eemaan* is of levels. It is of degrees and forever fluctuating. This is a matter that a person can witness in himself: when he is active and obedient, he senses a strength of *eemaan* and when he is falling short of the mark and disobeying Allaah he feels that his *eemaan* is weak.

Anyhow, this discussion before you is not to establish the fact that *eemaan* is of parts and that it increases and decreases - the evidences that point to this fact in the Qur'aan and *Sunnah* are numerous - even though this matter is extremely important as there does exist amongst Muslims the belief that *eemaan* is something whole and solid, which is not made up of parts and that everyone holds the same *eemaan*. The severity of this corrupt belief can be comprehended when one realises that the holder of this belief will not therefore seek to find out the ways that will increase his *eemaan* in order to implement them and nor will he averse himself with the matters that can weaken his *eemaan* so that he can avoid them because of his lack of belief in the increase and decrease of *eemaan*! This person has therefore sealed this tremendous door and bars himself from entering to succeed in obedience and shun disobedience. This is exactly what happened to the groups who held such a belief. One group held that since *eemaan* does not increase and decrease, actions do not affect it and hence, they concluded that sins have no bearing upon one's *eemaan* whatsoever. Another group did hold that *eemaan* is affected by action but as they again did not recognise that it was of levels and parts, they held that a person who commits a major sin is no longer a Muslim and he will reside in the Fire forever since his *eemaan* completely vanishes on account of the sin as it cannot decrease! Look at how *Shaytaan* deceives and plots against humankind to drive them towards disobedience in belief and action, we seek Allaah's protection from the constant bombardment of his whispers.

The discussion before you is directly connected to practical issues that relate to this subject: How does one actually increase in his *eemaan*? How can one safeguard himself from those matters that would otherwise weaken his *eemaan*? It is indeed a lofty discussion, which calls out to its reader to comprehend and implement it

The author of this excellent discussion is Shaykh 'Abdur-Razzaaq, the son of the illustrious scholar, Shaykh 'Abdul-Muhsin Ibn Hamad al-'Abbaad al-Badr who is one of the scholars of *al-Madeenah an-Nabawiyyah* and a lecturer at the Prophet's (ﷺ) mosque, may Allaah preserve them both. Shaykh 'Abdur-Razzaaq himself is a distinguished person of knowledge and he is an associate professor at the Department of 'Aqeedah in the Faculty of Da'wah and Usool ad-Deen at the Islamic University in al-Madeenah.

As the book before you is actually a single chapter - the third - from the Author's original work, a short preliminary discussion on the correct conception of *eemaan* - discussed by the author in the first chapter - is therefore most befitting to be outlined here. The necessity for this is further appreciated when one understands that the translation of *eemaan* as faith is insufficient and only covers half of its meaning. I will summarise certain points found in the original work and elsewhere, which should help one towards the correct understanding of the term *eemaan*.

1. Lexically, let alone from the *Sharee'ah* viewpoint, *eemaan* is not synonymous with *tasdeeq* (belief or faith).

2. It is much closer in meaning to the word *iqraar*, which embodies the belief of the heart, which is *tasdeeq* as well as the action of the heart, which is *inqiyaad* (compliance and submissiveness).

3. One can understand this even more so if he were to examine the contents of the *Sharee'ah*. The scrutiniser will find that it consists of two categories: (*khabr*) information and (*amr*) command. When Allaah tells us in the Qur'aan that we will be raised up after we die and that we will face him, this is information and one responds to it with belief in the heart (*tasdeeq*). However, when Allaah orders us to fast the month of Ramadaan, we do not respond by saying: "Yes, we believe". Rather, what is required is compliance, since this is a command. The compliance intended here is the willingness in the heart to accept the command and enact it. It is inconceivable for someone to actually remain holding *eemaan* if his heart is void of any willingness to obey the commands of Allaah. Whether the actual obedience takes place or not is not the issue here*, what is intended here, is the minimal level of compliance for *eemaan* to exist, which is the general willingness of the heart to enact the commands; to want to obey Allaah.

4. *Eemaan* has a core or basic level, which if it is not in the heart, then *eemaan* cannot exist in such a heart. The last point is exactly this basic level: the belief of the heart and the basic levels of certain actions of the heart, such as the minimal level of compliance, love of Allaah, fear of Allaah, hope in Allaah and so on. Added to this, is the articulation by the tongue of the *Shahaadah* for the one who wishes to embrace Islaam and has the ability to speak. The reasons and wisdom behind this ruling are beyond the scope of this brief discussion. This type of *eemaan* is what is termed as being a condition for the correctness and validity of *eemaan*.

5. *Eemaan* has higher parts and levels, above the core level. This is where those who possess *eemaan* become of different ranks and this is where the increase and decrease occurs. Hence, with regard to the actions of the heart, some have a greater love of Allaah than

* The issue of not praying is seen to be an exception here to those of the noble scholars who hold that it is a requirement for the establishment of the basis of *eemaan*. Indeed, it is a serious issue where a difference of opinion is present and Allaah knows best, therefore pray my brother and sister so that you come away from the point of contention.

others, while others fear him more and rely on him more. Others are superior in their sincerity and glorification of Allaah in their hearts and so on. Again, concerning the actions of the tongue, some recite Qur'aan more than others, some engage in much remembrance, speak only good etc. Likewise, people differ in the actions of the limbs: some pray *tahajjud*, perform *jihaad* etc in contrast to others. This type of *eemaan* is what is termed as being a condition for the perfection of one's *eemaan*.

6. *Eemaan* in the *Sharee'ah* is defined how the Prophet (ﷺ) defined it when questioned by Jibraa'eel: *Eemaan* in Allaah, the Angels, the Books, the Messengers, the Last Day and al-Qadar. As for the nature of *eemaan* and where it manifests itself, this is where the scholars have defined it with five important matters: it manifests itself in the heart, the tongue and upon the limbs and it increases and decreases.

7. Lastly, know that a misconception or error concerning the term *eemaan* is not like any other error concerning most other terms, because the rulings of this world and the Hereafter are connected to the terms of *eemaan*, Islaam, *kufr*, *nifaaq* etc. This important field of study which embodies all of this is referred to by some of the scholars as *Baab al-Asmaa wa al-Ahkaam* (the field of names and rulings) and Allaah knows best.

Points to note:

- The arabic original *'Asbaab Ziyaadah al-Eemaan wa Nuqsaanih'* is published by Daar al-Qalam wa al-Kitaab, 1414H, Riyadh.

- Translation of the Qur'aan is based on 'The Noble Qur'an' by Dr. Muhammad Taqi-ud-Din Al-Hilali and Dr. Muhammad Muhsin Khan with slight modification where necessary.

- Certain Arabic words have been transliterated and their meanings can be found in the glossary.

- May Allaah reward all those who have helped in this translation and with Him lies all success. May He make our actions sincerely for His Face and not let anyone have a share in them.

Introduction

All praise is for Allaah. We praise Him and seek His help and forgiveness. We turn to him in repentance and seek refuge in Allaah from the evil of our selves and the wickedness of our own deeds. Whomsoever Allaah guides, cannot be lead astray and whomsoever Allaah misguides, none can guide him. I bear witness that none has the right to be worshipped except Allaah, alone without any partner, and I bear witness that Muhammad is His slave and Messenger. May Allaah praise and send much peace upon him and all of his Companions.

The lofty rank and high station *eemaan* possesses is not something obscure, as it is unquestionably, the most important duty as well as being the most imperative of all obligations. It is also the greatest and most glorious of them. All the good in the world and the Hereafter is dependent upon the presence of *eemaan* and on its soundness and integrity.

Eemaan holds such a multitude of benefits, ripe fruits, delicious produce, constant food and continual goodness.

It is within this context, that those certain folk embarked upon and competed with each other in directing their attention to trying to actualise and fulfil *eemaan*. For the Muslim who is granted the *tawfeeq*, his concern for his *eemaan* is greater than any other concern he may have - and this must be so. When this became evident to the *Salaf* of this *ummah*, the first and best of this *ummah*, their concern for their *eemaan* was very eminent and the attention they gave to it was enormous.

They, may Allaah be pleased and have mercy upon them, used to tend to their *eemaan*, inspect their actions, and give each other advice. Reports of this nature from the *Salaf* are numerous:

1. 'Umar Ibn al-Khattaab, may Allaah be pleased with him, used to say to his companions: "Come on, so that we may increase our *eemaan*."

2. 'Abdullaah Ibn Mas'ood, may Allaah be pleased with him, used to say: "Sit with us, so that we may increase in *eemaan*." He used to say in his supplications: "O Allaah increase me in *eemaan*, certainty and understanding."

3. Mu'aadh Ibn Jabal, may Allaah be pleased with him, used to say: "Sit with us, so that we may have *eemaan* for an hour."

4. 'Abdullaah Ibn Rawaahah, may Allaah be pleased with him, used to take some of his companions by the hand and say: "Come on, so that we may have *eemaan* for an hour. Come on, let us remember Allaah so that we increase in *eemaan* by obeying him; He may remember us by forgiving us."

5. Aboo Dardaa', may Allaah be pleased with him, used to say: "It is from the intelligence of the servant to know whether he is increasing or decreasing, and indeed, it is from the intelligence of the servant to know how, where and when the whispers of *Shaytaan* appear to him."

6. 'Umayr Ibn Habeeb al-Khatmee, may Allaah be pleased with him, used to say: "*Eemaan* increases and decreases." Someone asked: "What increases it and what decreases it?" He replied: "If we remember Allaah (عَزَّ وَجَلَّ), praise Him, and declare His perfection; that is what increases it. If we are heedless, squander and forget; that is what decreases it."

7. 'Alqamah Ibn Qays an-Nakha'ee, may Allaah have mercy upon him, who is one of the senior and revered of the *taabi'een*, used to say to his companions: "Come with us, so that we may increase in *eemaan*."

8. 'Abdur-Rahmaan Ibn 'Amr al-Awzaa'ee, may Allaah have mercy upon him, was asked about *eemaan*: "Does it increase?" He replied, 'Yes, until it becomes like mountains. He was then asked,

'Does it decrease?' He answered, 'Yes, up until there is nothing left of it.'

9. The Imaam of the *Ahl as-Sunnah*, Ahmad Ibn Hanbal, may Allaah have mercy upon him, was asked as to whether *eemaan* increases and decreases. He replied: "It increases until it reaches the highest part of the seventh heaven, and it decreases until it reaches the lowest part of the seventh plane."

   He also used to say: "*Eemaan* is speech and action. It increases and decreases. If you perform good deeds, it increases, and if you do wrong, it decreases."

Narratives of this sort from them are numerous.

If one also reflects on their biographies and reads their tales, one will notice the intense concern they attached to the issue of *eemaan* and the great attention they gave to it.

These virtuous people knew that *eemaan* has many causes, which increase it, strengthen it, and make it grow, and likewise, that it has several other causes, which decrease it, weaken it and undermine it.

Accordingly, they strove to comply with that which strengthens and completes the *eemaan* and they warned, very strongly, against everything that weakened and decreased the *eemaan*. Thus, they became as a result, a righteous and virtuous people.

The knowledge therefore, of these causes, i.e., causes for the increase and decrease of *eemaan*, entails great and abundant benefits.

In fact, the knowledge and personification of these causes and focusing on them is of dire necessity. This is because *eemaan* signifies perfection for the servant, and it is the way towards his success and happiness. By *eemaan*, the servant's rank rises in this world and the Hereafter. It is the reason and route to all worldly and heavenly good, and it does not come about, obtain strength, or become complete, without knowledge of it's ways and causes.

Hence, it is very appropriate for the Muslim servant, the adviser to his own self and the one eager over his own happiness, to strive to acquaint himself with these causes. He should ponder over them and then apply them in his life, so that his *eemaan* increases and his certainty strengthens. He must also distance himself from the causes that decrease *eemaan*, and safeguard his self from committing them, so that he delivers himself from their ill end and painful consequences. The one who is granted the *tawfeeq* to this has indeed been given the *tawfeeq* to all good.

The great scholar Ibn Sa'dee, may Allaah (تعالى) have mercy upon him, says, 'The servant, Muslim, who has been granted the *tawfeeq*, does not cease from working towards two things:

The first, fulfilling *eemaan* and its subsidiaries, and establishing it in speech, action and state.

The second, striving to repel the apparent and hidden forms of *fitan,* which negate, invalidate or decrease *eemaan*.

The Muslim employs sincere repentance as a remedy for the shortcomings he has in the first matter as well as for that (i.e., the *fitan*) which he boldly embarked upon in the second matter, in addition to taking steps to make amends before it is too late.'[1]

Hence, the discussion before you contains an explanation and clarification of the most important causes for the increase and decrease of *eemaan*. The origin of this study is a chapter from my work *Ziyaadah al-Eemaan wa Nuqsaanuh, wa Hukm al-Istithnaa' Feeh.*[2] A number of exceptional individuals requested that it should be specifically separated and selected for publication in order for the benefit of all. Thus, it came to be, by the praise, favour and *tawfeeq* granted by Allaah. It is Allaah alone, that I ask for good intention and His acceptance and pleasure.

---

[1] *At-Tawdeeh wa al-Bayaan li Shajarah al-Eemaan*, page 38.

[2] It is currently in press. (It has since been published by *Maktabah Daar al-Qalam wa al-Kitaab*, Riyaadh, K.S.A. [t])

Causes for the Increase of *Eemaan*

Allaah (سبحانه) has set a cause and a way, with which, one arrives at anything desired and anything sought after. For a surety, the greatest of all pursuits and the one that holds the most extensive of benefits, is none other than *eemaan*. Allaah has devised many constituents for it that bring it about and strengthen it, and many causes that increase and develop it. If the servants act on them, their certainty strengthens and their *eemaan* increases. Allaah has elaborated on these in His Book, as has His Messenger (ﷺ) in his *Sunnah*. Possibly, the more important of these causes are the following:

1. Learning the Beneficial Knowledge Derived From the Book of Allaah and the *Sunnah* of His Messenger ﷺ

Ibn Rajab defines this knowledge, saying: "Beneficial knowledge is to define, accurately and meticulously, the texts of the Book and *Sunnah* and to understand them.

It is to confine oneself, in regard to this, to the reports transmitted from the Companions, their successors and their successors in turn, which pertain to the explanation and understanding of the Qur'aan and *hadeeths*, as well as the discourse related from them on issues of the lawful, unlawful, *zuhd* (i.e., asceticism), *raqaa'iq* (i.e., matters that soften the heart), the (various) branches of knowledge and so on.

It is also, to firstly, exert efforts towards distinguishing the authentic reports from the unauthentic, then secondly, to exert efforts towards seeking out their meanings and gaining an understanding of them. This is sufficient for the intelligent and (enough) labour for the one who is concerned and preoccupies himself with the beneficial knowledge..."[3]

---

[3] *Fadl 'Ilm as-Salaf 'alaa 'Ilm al-Khalaf*, page 45.

Whoever has been granted the *tawfeeq* to this knowledge has been granted the *tawfeeq* to the greatest cause for the increase of *eemaan*. Anyone who contemplates on the texts of the Book and *Sunnah* will realise this:

Allaah (تعالى) says:

شَهِدَ ٱللَّهُ أَنَّهُۥ لَآ إِلَٰهَ إِلَّا هُوَ وَٱلْمَلَٰٓئِكَةُ وَأُو۟لُوا۟ ٱلْعِلْمِ قَآئِمًۢا بِٱلْقِسْطِ ۚ

> **"Allaah bears witness that none deserves the right to be worshipped but He, and the Angels and those having knowledge (also give this witness); (He is always) maintaining His creation with justice..."**[4]

Allaah (تعالى) says:

لَّٰكِنِ ٱلرَّٰسِخُونَ فِى ٱلْعِلْمِ مِنْهُمْ وَٱلْمُؤْمِنُونَ يُؤْمِنُونَ بِمَآ أُنزِلَ إِلَيْكَ وَمَآ
أُنزِلَ مِن قَبْلِكَ ۚ وَٱلْمُقِيمِينَ ٱلصَّلَوٰةَ ۚ وَٱلْمُؤْتُونَ ٱلزَّكَوٰةَ
وَٱلْمُؤْمِنُونَ بِٱللَّهِ وَٱلْيَوْمِ ٱلْءَاخِرِ أُو۟لَٰٓئِكَ سَنُؤْتِيهِمْ أَجْرًا عَظِيمًا ﴿١٦٢﴾

> **"But those among them who are well-grounded in knowledge and the believers, believe in what has been sent down to you and in what was sent down before you, and those who establish prayer and give *zakaah* and believe in Allaah and the Last day, it is they to whom we shall give a great reward."**[5]

Allaah (تعالى) says:

إِنَّ ٱلَّذِينَ أُوتُوا۟ ٱلْعِلْمَ مِن قَبْلِهِۦٓ إِذَا يُتْلَىٰ
عَلَيْهِمْ يَخِرُّونَ لِلْأَذْقَانِ سُجَّدًا ﴿١٠٧﴾ وَيَقُولُونَ سُبْحَٰنَ رَبِّنَآ إِن كَانَ
وَعْدُ رَبِّنَا لَمَفْعُولًا ﴿١٠٨﴾ وَيَخِرُّونَ لِلْأَذْقَانِ يَبْكُونَ وَيَزِيدُهُمْ
خُشُوعًا ۩ ﴿١٠٩﴾

[4] Soorah Aal-'Imraan (3):18.

[5] Soorah an-Nisaa' (4):162.

> **"Verily, those who were given knowledge before it, when it is recited to them, fall down on their faces in humble prostration. And they say, 'How perfect is our Lord! Truly, the promise of our Lord must be fulfilled.' And they fall down on their faces weeping and it adds to their humility."**[6]

Allaah (تعالى) says:

> **"And that those who have been given knowledge may know that it (i.e., the Qur'aan) is the truth from your Lord, and that they may believe therein, and their hearts may submit to it with humility. And verily, Allaah is the Guide of those who believe, to the straight path."**[7]

Allaah (تعالى) says:

وَيَرَى ٱلَّذِينَ أُوتُوا۟ ٱلْعِلْمَ
ٱلَّذِىٓ أُنزِلَ إِلَيْكَ مِن رَّبِّكَ هُوَ ٱلْحَقَّ وَيَهْدِىٓ إِلَىٰ صِرَٰطِ
ٱلْعَزِيزِ ٱلْحَمِيدِ ﴿٦﴾

> **"And those who have been given knowledge see that what is revealed to you from your Lord is the truth, and that it guides to the path of the Exalted in might, Owner of all praise."**[8]

---

[6] Soorah al-Israa' (17):107-109.

[7] Soorah al-Hajj (22):54.

[8] Soorah Saba' (34):6.

Allaah (تعالى) says:

إِنَّمَا يَخْشَى ٱللَّهَ مِنْ عِبَادِهِ ٱلْعُلَمَٰٓؤُا۟ ۗ إِنَّ ٱللَّهَ عَزِيزٌ غَفُورٌ ﴿٢٨﴾

"It is only those who have knowledge amongst His slaves who fear Allaah. Verily, Allaah is All-Mighty, Oft-Forgiving."[9]

Allaah (تعالى) says:

يَرْفَعِ ٱللَّهُ ٱلَّذِينَ ءَامَنُوا۟
مِنكُمْ وَٱلَّذِينَ أُوتُوا۟ ٱلْعِلْمَ دَرَجَٰتٍ ۚ وَٱللَّهُ بِمَا تَعْمَلُونَ خَبِيرٌ ﴿١١﴾

"Allaah will exalt in degree those of you who believe, and those who have been granted knowledge. And Allaah is well acquainted with what you do."[10]

Recorded in the *Saheehayn*, is the *hadeeth* of Mu'aawiyah, may Allaah be pleased with him, in which he says, 'The Messenger of Allaah (ﷺ) said: *"Whomever Allaah desires good for, He imparts upon him understanding of the religion."*'[11]

Related in *al-Musnad* and other sources, is the *hadeeth* of Aboo ad-Dardaa', may Allaah be pleased with him, in which he says, 'The Messenger of Allaah (ﷺ) said: *"He who treads a path in search of knowledge, Allaah will direct him to tread a path from the paths of Paradise. The Angels lower their wings for the student of knowledge in approval of what he does. All in the heavens and earth and the fish in the depth of the water seek forgiveness for the scholar, and the superiority of the scholar over the worshipper is like the superiority of the full moon at night over the rest of the stars. Verily, the scholars are the heirs to the Prophets. Verily, the Prophets did not bequeath deenars or dirhams. All they left behind was knowledge, so whoever takes it, has indeed acquired a huge fortune."*'[12]

---

[9] Soorah Faatir (35):28.

[10] Soorah al-Mujaadilah (58):11.

[11] Related by al-Bukhaaree, (1/164, 6/217, 12,294 *Fath*) and Muslim, 4/1524.

[12] *Al-Musnad*, 5/196. Also related by Aboo Daawood, 3/317; at-Tirmidhee, 5/49; Ibn Maajah 1/81; ad-Daarimee, 1/98 and Ibn Hibbaan, 1/152 (*al-Ihsaan*). It was declared *saheeh* by al-Albaanee; see *Saheeh al-Jaami'* 5/302. Ibn Rajab has provided a commentary to this *hadeeth* in a small work of his, so one should refer to it.

In at-Tirmidhee and other sources, is the *hadeeth* of Aboo Umaamah, may Allaah be pleased with him, in which he says, 'The Messenger of Allaah (ﷺ) said: *"The excellence of the scholar over the worshipper is like my excellence over the lowermost of you. Indeed, Allaah (ﷻ), His Angels, the inhabitants of the heavens and earth, even the ant in its hole and the fish, supplicate for one who teaches good to the people."*'[13]

The aforementioned texts manifest the rank and status of knowledge, and its great standing and importance. They also show the commendable effects and noble qualities in this world and the Hereafter, which are a consequence of knowledge, as well as the results they bear, such as humility and submission to the Laws of Allaah and compliance and adherence to His commands.

Thus, the scholar knows his Lord, his Prophet and the commands and boundaries set by Allaah. He distinguishes between that which Allaah loves and is pleased with, and that which He hates and rejects. Thus, he acts in accordance to the commands of Allaah with respect to that which he approaches and refrains from.

This is true for the one who is given the *tawfeeq* towards acting upon that which he knows, if however, the case is the opposite, his knowledge will be a curse for him.

Al-Aajurree states in the introduction to his book *Akhlaaq al-'Ulamaa'*: "Allaah (ﷻ), sanctified are His names, singled out those of His creation whom He loved and then guided them to *eemaan*. He further singled out from amongst the believers those whom He loved and favoured them by teaching them the Book and *Hikmah*.

He granted them the *tawfeeq* in the religion, taught them the explanation and favoured them over the rest of the believers. This is the case in every age and place. Allaah elevated them with knowledge and adorned them with forbearance. Through them, the lawful is known from the unlawful, the truth from falsehood, the harmful from the beneficial, and the good from the bad.

[13] Related by at-Tirmidhee, 5/50. Al-Mundharee mentioned it in *at-Targheeb wa at-Tarheeb* 1/101 and he related from at-Tirmidhee that he said: "The *hadeeth* is *hasan saheeh*." It has been declared *saheeh* by al-Albaanee, see *Saheeh at-Tirmidhee*, 2/343.

Their virtue is enormous and their standing is great. They are the heirs to the Prophets and a pleasure to the eyes of the righteous. The fish in the sea seek forgiveness for them, the Angels lower their wings for them and they are second after the Prophets who will intercede on the (Day of) Resurrection. Their gatherings impart wisdom. Through their actions, the heedless are restrained and scolded.

They are the best of the slaves and are higher in rank than the *zuhaad* (i.e., ascetics). Their life is a treasure and their death is a calamity. They remind the negligent and enlighten the ignorant. Trouble and ill treatment is not expected or feared from them. By their fine instruction, the obedient ones dispute and by their eloquent sermon, the slack ones return. Everyone is in need of their knowledge... so they are the lamps for the servants, the landmarks of communities, the backbone of the *ummah*, and the sources of wisdom. They are the subject of *Shaytaan's* rage. Because of them, the hearts of the people of truth come to life and the hearts of the people of deviation die.

Their similitude upon this earth is that of the stars; they guide one in the darkness of the land and sea. If the stars blacken out, people become confused and when the darkness unveils the stars, they see."[14]

Al-Aajurree then related texts from the Book and *Sunnah*, as well as statements of the people of knowledge, which support what he mentioned.

Thus, knowledge possesses a lofty rank and a very high status. Knowledge has only been granted this great status, as it is a means to the greatest of all aims: that is the worship of Allaah (تعالى) alone, without any partner, and the establishment of *tawheed* of Him in the required way.

Knowledge is therefore, not sought after in itself but for something else,[15] and that is action. Consequently, every type of knowledge within

---

[14] *Ahklaaq al-'Ulamaa*, page 13 & 14.

[15] **Publisher's Note:** From a more detailed discussion of this issue refer to *Adorning Knowledge with Actions* by Shaykh Husayn al-'Awaayishah (Al-Hidaayah Publishing and Distribution, UK, 1999).

the *Sharee'ah* that the law of Islaam calls for, is demanded because it is a means to the worship of Allaah (تعالى) and for no other reason. This is proven by the following facts:

The first: The *sharee'ah* has not brought anything but worship, this is the reason behind the dispatching of the Prophets (*'alayhim as-salaam*). Allaah (تعالى) says:

يَٰٓأَيُّهَا ٱلنَّاسُ ٱعْبُدُوا۟ رَبَّكُمُ

"O Mankind! Worship your Lord..."[16]

Allaah (تعالى) says:

الٓر ۚ كِتَٰبٌ أُحْكِمَتْ ءَايَٰتُهُۥ ثُمَّ فُصِّلَتْ مِن لَّدُنْ حَكِيمٍ خَبِيرٍ ﴿١﴾
أَلَّا تَعْبُدُوٓا۟ إِلَّا ٱللَّهَ ۚ

"*Alif Laam Raa*. (This is) a Book, the *aayaat* whereof are perfected, and then explained in detail from One who is All-Wise and Well-Acquainted, that you worship none but Allaah..."[17]

Allaah says:

وَمَآ أَرْسَلْنَا مِن قَبْلِكَ مِن رَّسُولٍ إِلَّا نُوحِىٓ إِلَيْهِ أَنَّهُۥ لَآ إِلَٰهَ
إِلَّآ أَنَا۠ فَٱعْبُدُونِ ﴿٢٥﴾

"And We did not send any messenger before you but We inspired him (saying), 'None has the right to be worshipped but I, so worship Me (alone)'."[18]

Allaah says:

إِنَّآ أَنزَلْنَآ إِلَيْكَ ٱلْكِتَٰبَ بِٱلْحَقِّ فَٱعْبُدِ ٱللَّهَ مُخْلِصًا
لَّهُ ٱلدِّينَ ﴿٢﴾ أَلَا لِلَّهِ ٱلدِّينُ ٱلْخَالِصُ ۚ

---

[16] Soorah al-Baqarah (2):21.

[17] Soorah Hood (11):1-2.

[18] Soorah al-Anbiyaa (21):25.

> **"Verily We have sent down the Book to you in truth. So, worship Allaah by making your religion sincerely for Him alone. Surely, to Allaah alone belongs the sincere religion..."**[19]

Likewise, there are so many other *aayaat* that cannot easily be enumerated without some effort. They all point towards the fact that the intention behind knowledge is worship of Allaah (ﷻ) and to direct all acts of worship and obedience to Him.

The second: The evidences that indicate the spirit of knowledge to be action and that without action, knowledge is bare and of no benefit.

Allaah (تعالى) has said:

إِنَّمَا يَخْشَى ٱللَّهَ مِنْ عِبَادِهِ ٱلْعُلَمَٰٓؤُا۟

> **"...It is only those who have knowledge amongst His slaves who fear Allaah..."**[20]

Allaah (تعالى) says:

أَمَّنْ هُوَ قَٰنِتٌ ءَانَآءَ ٱلَّيْلِ سَاجِدًا وَقَآئِمًا يَحْذَرُ
ٱلْءَاخِرَةَ وَيَرْجُوا۟ رَحْمَةَ رَبِّهِۦ ۗ قُلْ هَلْ يَسْتَوِى ٱلَّذِينَ يَعْلَمُونَ وَٱلَّذِينَ
لَا يَعْلَمُونَ ۗ إِنَّمَا يَتَذَكَّرُ أُو۟لُوا۟ ٱلْأَلْبَٰبِ ﴿٩﴾

> **"Is one who is obedient to Allaah, prostrating himself or standing (in prayer) during the hours of the night, fearing the Hereafter and hoping for the Mercy of his Lord (like one who disbelieves)? Say, 'Are those who know equal to those who know not?' It is only people of understanding who will remember."**[21]

These and other evidences show that knowledge is a particular type of means and is not in the view of the *Sharee'ah*, sought after in itself. It is none other than the way to action. Furthermore, all the reports

---

[19] Soorah az-Zumar (39):2-3.

[20] Soorah al-Faaṯir (35):28.

[21] Soorah az-Zumar (39):9.

related on the excellence of knowledge are only established from the perspective that the person is obliged to act upon this knowledge.

It is of common fact that the best branch of knowledge is knowledge of Allaah (عَزَّ وَجَلَّ). Nevertheless, this knowledge is not regarded a virtue for it's holder unless he remains true to its dictates and that is (to actually possess) *eemaan* in Allaah.

The third: The severe warnings, threats and harsh reprimands mentioned in the texts of the *Sharee'ah* for the one who does not act in accordance to his knowledge. The fact that the scholar will be questioned on what he did with his knowledge, and that it will be a source of grievance, regret and (the) curse (of Allaah) for the one who does not act upon it.

Allaah (تعالى) says:

أَتَأْمُرُونَ ٱلنَّاسَ بِٱلْبِرِّ
وَتَنسَوْنَ أَنفُسَكُمْ وَأَنتُمْ تَتْلُونَ ٱلْكِتَٰبَ ۚ أَفَلَا تَعْقِلُونَ ﴿٤٤﴾

"Do you enjoin righteousness upon the people and forget yourselves (to practise it) whilst you recite the scripture? Have you then no sense?"[22]

Allaah (تعالى) says:

يَٰٓأَيُّهَا ٱلَّذِينَ ءَامَنُوا۟ لِمَ تَقُولُونَ مَا لَا تَفْعَلُونَ ﴿٢﴾
كَبُرَ مَقْتًا عِندَ ٱللَّهِ أَن تَقُولُوا۟ مَا لَا تَفْعَلُونَ ﴿٣﴾

"O you who believe! Why do you say that which you do not do? Most hateful it is with Allaah that you say that which you do not do."[23]

[22] Soorah al-Baqarah (2):44.

[23] Soorah a<u>s</u>-<u>S</u>aff (61):2-3.

Allaah (تعالى) says relating what Shu'ayb declared to his community:

> **"...I wish not to contradict you and do that which I forbid you. I only desire reform as far as I am able to do so, and my *tawfeeq* cannot come about except by Allaah. In Him I trust and Unto Him I repent."**[24]

There are many other texts of this nature. In addition, there exists numerous reports from the *Salaf* on this issue, they are of great benefit and sublime value, scholars have related and passed on these reports in their works.[25]

Shaykh al-Islaam Ibn Taymiyyah states: "...this is why it is said, 'Knowledge is of two types: knowledge in the heart and knowledge upon the tongue. The knowledge in the heart is the beneficial knowledge and the knowledge upon the tongue is the proof of Allaah upon His slaves'[26]...so the *faqeeh* whose heart has acquired understanding and enlightenment is not like the *khateeb* who addresses with his tongue. The heart may attain great matters of knowledge and understanding and its occupier may not speak of it to anyone. Similarly, one may speak about many issues concerning the heart and its states and the person may be at the same time void and bare of such matters."[27]

By what has preceded, one can now comprehend the rank and status knowledge possesses as well as its immense benefits and returns.

---

[24] Soorah Hood (11):88.

[25] Refer to some of these statements in al-Khateeb al-Baghdaadee's work, *Iqtidaa' al-'Ilm al-'Amal* and the treatise by al-Haafidh Ibn 'Asaakir, *Dhamm man laa ya'mal bi 'Ilmih*. Both works are published.

[26] This is a statement of al-Hasan al-Basree, may Allaah have mercy upon him, and it is recorded by ad-Daarimee (1/102). Shaykh al-Islaam mentioned this in *al-Fataawa* and attributed it to al-Hasan, see: 7/23.

[27] *Dar' at-Ta'aarud* 7/453-454.

One can apprehend the powerful effect it has on the strength and steadfastness of *eemaan*, and the fact that it is the greatest cause for the increase, growth and strength of *eemaan*. This holds true for the one who acts in accordance with this knowledge.

In fact, actions themselves differ, with respect to their increase, decrease, acceptance and rejection, in proportion to their agreement and conformity to knowledge. Ibn al-Qayyim, may Allaah have mercy upon him, mentioned this: "Actions differ with respect to acceptance and rejection in proportion to their agreement or opposition to knowledge. Thus, the action that conforms to knowledge is the acceptable type, whereas, the action that opposes knowledge is the rejected type. Knowledge is the scale and it is the criterion."[28]

He also said: "Any knowledge or action that does not increase *eemaan* in strength is diseased..."[29]

The increase of *eemaan* brought about by knowledge is achieved in many ways: to travel in search of knowledge; to sit with people of knowledge in their gatherings; to study issues of knowledge in company; to increase in knowledge of Allaah and His *Sharee'ah*; to practise what one learns and as for those who acquire knowledge, there is a reward. These are some of the ways in which *eemaan* increases as a result of knowledge and its attainment.

As for the branches of *sharee'ah* knowledge that can cause an increase of *eemaan*, they are abundant. The following is a summarised selection of them:

i. Reciting the Noble Qur'aan and Contemplating on it

This is one of the greatest branches of knowledge that can lead to the increase, stability and strengthening of ee*maan*.

Allaah has revealed His lucid Book to His servants as a source of guidance; mercy, light and glad tidings and as a remembrance for those who remember.

[28] *Miftaah Daar as-Sa'aadah*, page 89.

[29] *Al-Fawaa'id*, page 162.

Allaah (تعالى) says:

وَهَٰذَا كِتَٰبٌ أَنزَلْنَٰهُ مُبَارَكٌ مُّصَدِّقُ ٱلَّذِى بَيْنَ يَدَيْهِ

"And this is a blessed Book that We have sent down, confirming that which came before it..."[30]

Allaah (تعالى) says:

وَهَٰذَا كِتَٰبٌ أَنزَلْنَٰهُ مُبَارَكٌ فَٱتَّبِعُوهُ وَٱتَّقُوا۟ لَعَلَّكُمْ تُرْحَمُونَ

"And this is a blessed Book that We have sent down, so follow it and fear (Allaah), that you may receive mercy."[31]

Allaah (تعالى) says:

وَلَقَدْ جِئْنَٰهُم بِكِتَٰبٍ فَصَّلْنَٰهُ عَلَىٰ عِلْمٍ هُدًى وَرَحْمَةً لِّقَوْمٍ يُؤْمِنُونَ

"Certainly, we have brought to them a Book, which we have explained in detail, upon knowledge, as a guidance and a mercy to a people who believe."[32]

Allaah (تعالى) says:

وَنَزَّلْنَا عَلَيْكَ ٱلْكِتَٰبَ تِبْيَٰنًا لِّكُلِّ شَىْءٍ وَهُدًى
وَرَحْمَةً وَبُشْرَىٰ لِلْمُسْلِمِينَ ﴿٨٩﴾

"...And We have sent down to you the Book, as a clarification of everything, a guidance, a mercy and as glad tidings for the Muslims."[33]

Allaah (تعالى) says:

كِتَٰبٌ أَنزَلْنَٰهُ إِلَيْكَ مُبَٰرَكٌ لِّيَدَّبَّرُوٓا۟ ءَايَٰتِهِۦ وَلِيَتَذَكَّرَ أُو۟لُوا۟ ٱلْأَلْبَٰبِ

"(This is a) Book that We have sent down to you, full of blessings, so that they may ponder over its *aayaat*, and that those of understanding may remember."[34]

---

[30] Soorah al-An'aam (6):92.

[31] Soorah al-An'aam (6):155.

[32] Soorah al-A'raaf (7):52.

[33] Soorah an-Nahl (16):89.

[34] Soorah Saad (38):29.

Allaah (تعالى) says:

إِنَّ هَٰذَا ٱلْقُرْءَانَ يَهْدِى لِلَّتِى هِىَ أَقْوَمُ وَيُبَشِّرُ
ٱلْمُؤْمِنِينَ ٱلَّذِينَ يَعْمَلُونَ ٱلصَّٰلِحَٰتِ أَنَّ لَهُمْ أَجْرًا كَبِيرًا ﴿٩﴾

"Verily, this Qur'aan guides to that which is most just and right, and gives glad tidings to the believers who work righteous deeds, that they shall have a great reward."[35]

Allaah (تعالى) says:

وَنُنَزِّلُ مِنَ ٱلْقُرْءَانِ مَا هُوَ شِفَآءٌ
وَرَحْمَةٌ لِّلْمُؤْمِنِينَ وَلَا يَزِيدُ ٱلظَّٰلِمِينَ إِلَّا خَسَارًا ﴿٨٢﴾

"And We send down of the Qur'aan that which is a healing and a mercy to those who believe, and it increases the oppressors in nothing but loss."[36]

Allaah (تعالى) says:

إِنَّ فِى ذَٰلِكَ لَذِكْرَىٰ لِمَن كَانَ
لَهُۥ قَلْبٌ أَوْ أَلْقَى ٱلسَّمْعَ وَهُوَ شَهِيدٌ ﴿٣٧﴾

"Verily, therein is indeed a reminder for him who has a heart or gives ear while he is heedful."[37]

These noble *aayaat* contain mention of the excellence of the Noble Qur'aan, the Book of the Lord of the Worlds. The fact that Allaah made it blessed and a guidance for the worlds. He placed within it a cure for illnesses, especially, the illnesses and diseases of misconceptions and desires of the heart. He made it a source of glad tidings and mercy for the worlds and as a form of remembrance for those who remember. He made it a guide towards that which is most just and upright, and He mentioned *aayaat* and threats by which they may fear or would cause them to remember and reflect.

[35] Soorah al-Israa (17):9.

[36] Soorah al-Israa (17):82.

[37] Soorah Qaaf (50):37.

Thus, one who reads the Qur'aan, and ponders and reflects over its *aayaat*, finds within it such knowledge and learning, which strengthen, increase and develop his *eemaan*.

This is because he will come across within the discourse of the Qur'aan, a King, who possesses all dominion, for whom alone, is all praise. The reigns of all affairs are in His hand alone, they emanate from Him and return to Him. He has ascended above His throne and not a single secret in the regions of His dominion escapes Him.

He is aware of what is in the souls of His slaves, fully cognisant of their hidden and public deeds. Solely, He disposes of the affairs of the Kingdom.

He hears and sees, gives and withholds, rewards and punishes, and honours and abases. He creates and sustains, and gives life and causes death. He decrees, executes and disposes.

He invites His servants and directs them towards what constitutes their happiness and success. He entices them towards this, and warns them of what will cause their ruin.

He introduces Himself to them by His names and attributes. He woos them with His favours and blessings and reminds them of His favours upon them. He commands them with what entitles them to the completion of such favours and blessings and warns them of His vengeance. He reminds them of the honour He has prepared for them if they obey Him, and of the punishment He has prepared for them if they disobey Him.

He informs them of how He handles His awliyaa' and His enemies, and of the outcome of both. He praises His *awliyaa'* for their righteous actions and fine qualities. He censures His enemies for their bad deeds and distasteful characteristics.

He puts forward parables and provides numerous types of proofs and truths. He replies to the misconceptions of His enemies with the finest of answers. He gives credit to the truthful and denies the liar. He speaks the truth and guides towards the path.

He invites to the abode of peace and safety (i.e., Paradise). He mentions its description, its beauty and its bliss. He warns against the abode of destruction (i.e., the Hellfire). He mentions its torment, its ugliness and its pains.

He reminds His slaves of their necessity towards Him, their dire need of Him, and that they can never be independent of Him even for the blink of an eyelid. He informs them that He can dispense of them and of all creation, and that He Himself is the Rich and is not dependent on anything, whereas, everything besides Him is inherently in need of Him.

He makes known to them, that no one attains an atom's worth or more of good except by His Favour and Mercy, and that no one attains an atom's worth or more of bad except by His justice and wisdom. One witnesses from His speech, His reproach of His beloved in the most gracious of ways and despite that, He dismisses their mistakes and forgives their slips. He accredits their excuses, rectifies their corruption, defends and protects them. He is their victor, their guardian over their welfare and the one who delivers them from all difficulties. He is the One who will keep His promise to them, He is their only patron and protector. He is their true patron and protector and their victor over their enemies. How fine a patron and victor He is!

Hence, the servant never ceases to benefit from reflecting on the Book of Allaah. His heart bears witness to such types of knowledge that increase his *eemaan* and strengthen it.

How can this not be so? When he finds within the Qur'aan, a King who is glorious, merciful, generous and beautiful; this is His standing.

So how can he not love Him, compete to attain a nearness to Him or use up his energy in trying to show love for Him?

How can He not be more beloved to him than anything else? How can he not prefer His pleasure to anyone else's pleasure?

How can he not be attached to His remembrance? How can his love for Him, his desire to meet Him and feeling close to Him not be his nourishment, strength and medicine, in that if he were to be bereft of this, he would become corrupt and ruined and would not benefit from his life?[38]

Al-Aajurree, may Allaah have mercy upon him, said: "Whoever contemplates His words, will know the Lord (عَزَّ وَجَلَّ) and he will know of His great power and capability, His immense favour upon the believers, and of the obligation upon himself to worship Him.

Accordingly, the person imposes this duty upon himself thereby being on his guard against that which his Generous Patron and Protector has warned of and coveting that which He has made desirous.

Whoever is of this description when reciting the Qur'aan or when listening to it when recited by another, the Qur'aan will be a cure for him. He becomes rich without money, he attains power and strength without kinsfolk and finds intimacy in that which others feel alienation towards.

His desire when opening a *Soorah* for recitation will be, 'when will I accede to the admonition contained within what I recite?' and his desire will not be, 'when will I complete this *Soorah*?'

His aspiration is none other than, 'When will I understand what Allaah is addressing me with? When will I restrain (from committing sins)? When will I take heed?'

This is because reciting the Qur'aan is worship and it is not to be done so in a state of heedlessness, and Allaah is the one who grants the *tawfeeq* towards that."[39]

For this reason, Allaah, the Generous, orders His servants and encourages them to ponder over the Qur'aan, Allaah (سبحانه) says:

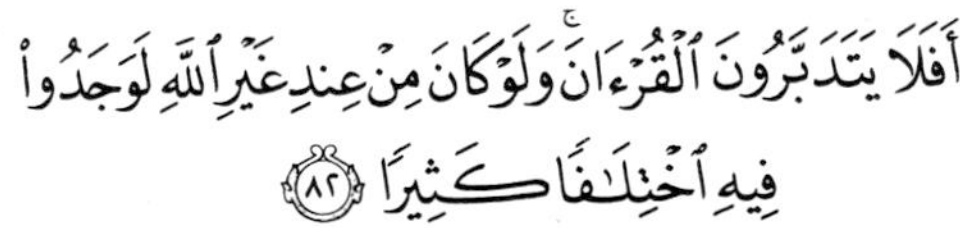

[38] Refer to *al-Fawaa'id* of Ibn al-Qayyim, pages 58-60.

[39] *Akhlaaq Hamlah al-Qur'aan*, by al-Aajurree, page 10.

"Do they not then contemplate on the Qur'aan? Had it been from other than Allaah, they would surely have found therein much contradiction."[40]

He says:

أَفَلَا يَتَدَبَّرُونَ ٱلْقُرْءَانَ أَمْ عَلَىٰ قُلُوبٍ أَقْفَالُهَآ ﴿٢٤﴾

"Do they not then contemplate on the Qur'aan, or are there locks upon their hearts?[41]

Allaah (سبحانه) proclaims that He only revealed the Qur'aan so that its *aayaat* would be pondered over, He says:

كِتَٰبٌ أَنزَلْنَٰهُ إِلَيْكَ مُبَٰرَكٌ لِّيَدَّبَّرُوٓا۟ ءَايَٰتِهِۦ وَلِيَتَذَكَّرَ أُو۟لُوا۟ ٱلْأَلْبَٰبِ

"(This is a) Book that We have sent down to you, full of blessings, so that they may ponder over its *aayaat*, and that those of understanding may remember."[42]

Allaah also explains that the reason behind the lack of guidance for the one who deviates from the straight path is his disregard for reflecting on the Qur'aan and being too proud to listen to it, He says:

قَدْ كَانَتْ ءَايَٰتِى
تُتْلَىٰ عَلَيْكُمْ فَكُنتُمْ عَلَىٰٓ أَعْقَٰبِكُمْ تَنكِصُونَ ﴿٦٦﴾ مُسْتَكْبِرِينَ
بِهِۦ سَٰمِرًا تَهْجُرُونَ ﴿٦٧﴾ أَفَلَمْ يَدَّبَّرُوا۟ ٱلْقَوْلَ أَمْ جَآءَهُم مَّا لَمْ يَأْتِ
ءَابَآءَهُمُ ٱلْأَوَّلِينَ ﴿٦٨﴾

"Indeed, My *aayaat* used to be recited to you, but you used to turn back on your heels. With haughtiness, you talked evil about it (i.e., the Qur'aan) throughout the night. Have they not then pondered over the Word (i.e., the Qur'aan) or has there come to them what had not come to their fathers of old?"[43]

---

[40] Soorah an-Nisaa' (4):82.

[41] Soorah Muhammad (47):24.

[42] Soorah Saad (38):29.

[43] Soorah al-Mu'minoon (23):66-68.

He (سبحانه) mentions of the Qur'aan that it increases the believers in *eemaan* if they read it and contemplate on its *aayaat*, Allaah (سبحانه) says:

إِنَّمَا ٱلْمُؤْمِنُونَ ٱلَّذِينَ إِذَا ذُكِرَ ٱللَّهُ وَجِلَتْ قُلُوبُهُمْ وَإِذَا تُلِيَتْ عَلَيْهِمْ ءَايَٰتُهُۥ زَادَتْهُمْ إِيمَٰنًا وَعَلَىٰ رَبِّهِمْ يَتَوَكَّلُونَ ﴿٢﴾

"The believers are none other than those whose hearts feel fear when Allaah is mentioned. When His *aayaat* are recited to them, they (i.e., the *aayaat*) increase them in their *eemaan* and upon their Lord (alone), they rely."[44]

Allaah relates about the righteous amongst the Ahl al-*Kitaab*, that when the Qur'aan is recited to them they fall upon their faces in humble prostration and in a state of weeping, and that it increases them in humility, *eemaan* and submission. Allaah (سبحانه) says:

قُلْ ءَامِنُوا۟ بِهِۦٓ أَوْ لَا تُؤْمِنُوٓا۟ ۚ إِنَّ ٱلَّذِينَ أُوتُوا۟ ٱلْعِلْمَ مِن قَبْلِهِۦٓ إِذَا يُتْلَىٰ عَلَيْهِمْ يَخِرُّونَ لِلْأَذْقَانِ سُجَّدًا ﴿١٠٧﴾ وَيَقُولُونَ سُبْحَٰنَ رَبِّنَآ إِن كَانَ وَعْدُ رَبِّنَا لَمَفْعُولًا ﴿١٠٨﴾ وَيَخِرُّونَ لِلْأَذْقَانِ يَبْكُونَ وَيَزِيدُهُمْ خُشُوعًا ۩ ﴿١٠٩﴾

"Say, 'Believe in it (i.e., the Qur'aan) or do not believe (in it). Verily, those who were given knowledge before it, when it is recited to them, they fall upon their faces in humble prostration, and they say: "How perfect is our Lord! Truly, the promise of our Lord will be fulfilled." They fall upon their faces weeping and it adds to their humility.'"[45]

He (سبحانه) also informs that if He were to send down the Glorious Qur'aan upon a mountain, it would humble itself and rupture because of the fear of Allaah (عزّ وجلّ). He made this as a parable for the people to demonstrate to them the greatness of the Qur'aan. He says:

---

[44] Soorah al-Anfaal (8):2.

[45] Soorah al-Israa' (17):107-109.

لَوْ أَنزَلْنَا هَٰذَا
ٱلْقُرْءَانَ عَلَىٰ جَبَلٍ لَّرَأَيْتَهُۥ خَٰشِعًا مُّتَصَدِّعًا مِّنْ خَشْيَةِ
ٱللَّهِ ۚ وَتِلْكَ ٱلْأَمْثَٰلُ نَضْرِبُهَا لِلنَّاسِ لَعَلَّهُمْ يَتَفَكَّرُونَ

"Had We sent down this Qur'aan on a mountain, you would surely have seen it humbling itself and rending asunder out of fear of Allaah. Such are the parables that We put forward to mankind that they may reflect."[46]

He described the Qur'aan as being the best of speech, parts of it resembling other parts and He repeated some of it so that it would be understood. He mentioned that the skins of the righteous shiver in fear and hope when they hear the Qur'aan. He says:

ٱللَّهُ نَزَّلَ أَحْسَنَ ٱلْحَدِيثِ كِتَٰبًا مُّتَشَٰبِهًا مَّثَانِىَ تَقْشَعِرُّ مِنْهُ
جُلُودُ ٱلَّذِينَ يَخْشَوْنَ رَبَّهُمْ ثُمَّ تَلِينُ جُلُودُهُمْ وَقُلُوبُهُمْ
إِلَىٰ ذِكْرِ ٱللَّهِ ۚ ذَٰلِكَ هُدَى ٱللَّهِ يَهْدِى بِهِۦ مَن يَشَآءُ ۚ وَمَن
يُضْلِلِ ٱللَّهُ فَمَا لَهُۥ مِنْ هَادٍ ﴿٢٣﴾

"Allaah has sent down the best speech, a Book, its parts resembling each other in goodness and truth, oft repeated. The skins of those who fear their Lord shiver from it. Thereafter, their skin and hearts soften to the remembrance of Allaah. That is the guidance of Allaah. He guides with it whom He pleases and whomever Allaah sends astray, has no guide whatsoever."[47]

Allaah censures the believers for their lack of humility when listening to the Qur'aan and He cautions them to not resemble the disbelievers in this regard. He says:

[46] Soorah al-Hashr (59):21.

[47] Soorah az-Zumar (39):23.

أَلَمْ يَأْنِ لِلَّذِينَ آمَنُوا أَن تَخْشَعَ قُلُوبُهُمْ لِذِكْرِ اللَّهِ
وَمَا نَزَلَ مِنَ الْحَقِّ وَلَا يَكُونُوا كَالَّذِينَ أُوتُوا الْكِتَابَ مِن قَبْلُ
فَطَالَ عَلَيْهِمُ الْأَمَدُ فَقَسَتْ قُلُوبُهُمْ ۖ وَكَثِيرٌ مِّنْهُمْ فَاسِقُونَ ﴿١٦﴾

"Has not the time come for the hearts of those who believe to be affected by Allaah's reminder (i.e., the Qur'aan) and of the truth that has been revealed, and not to be like those who had been given the Book before, whereby the term was lengthened for them and their hearts became hard and many of them are rebellious."[48]

These aforementioned *aayaat* contain the clearest indication of the importance of the Qur'aan, the required attention that has to be paid to it, its powerful effect upon the hearts, and that it is the greatest matter that increases *eemaan*, especially, if the recitation is performed upon contemplation, reflection and on trying to understand its meaning.

Ibn al-Qayyim, may Allaah have mercy upon him, says: "In short, there is nothing more beneficial for the heart than reading the Qur'aan with contemplation and reflection. The Qur'aan encompasses all the levels of the travellers, the conditions of the workers, and stations of those possessing knowledge. It is the Qur'aan that generates love, desire, fear, hope, repentance, reliance, pleasure, entrustment, gratitude, patience and the rest of the different states that are life to the heart and perfection of it. Likewise, it repels all the rebuked characteristics and actions that cause the corruption and ruin of the heart.

If people were to possess a realisation of what recitation of the Qur'aan with contemplation contains, they would devote themselves to it at the expense of anything else. When the person reads it with reflection and he comes across an *aayah* that he is in need of, for the cure of his heart, he repeats it, even if he does so a hundred times or the whole night. Hence, to recite a single *aayah* of the Qur'aan with contemplation and reflection is better than reciting the Qur'aan to com-

---

[48] Soorah al-Hadeed (57):16.

pletion without any contemplation or reflection. It is also more beneficial for the heart and more conducive to attaining *eemaan* and tasting the sweetness of the Qur'aan..."[49]

Mu<u>h</u>ammad Rasheed Ri<u>d</u>aa states: "Know that strength of religion and culmination of *eemaan* and certainty does not come about except by reading the Qur'aan very often and listening to it upon contemplation with the intention of being guided by it and to act on its commands and prohibitions. The correct and submissive *eemaan* increases, strengthens, develops and its effects such as righteous actions and abandonment of disobedience and corruption, all arise in proportion to the contemplation of the Qur'aan. It also decreases and weakens in proportion to not contemplating on the Qur'aan.

Most of the Arabs only believed when they heard the Qur'aan and understood it. They did not conquer the lands, inhabit cities, nor did their population grow and their power become greater except because of the Qur'aan's effective guidance.

Furthermore, the nobles of Makkah who opposed and stood in enmity, strove against the Prophet and tried to prevent him from conveying the message of his Lord by stopping him from reciting the Qur'aan to the people:

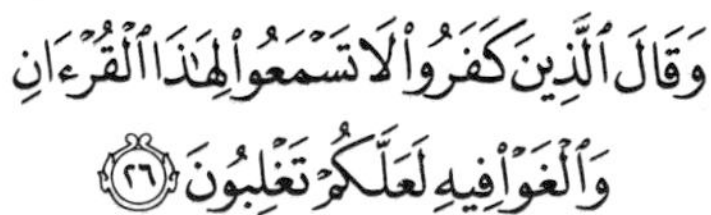

> **"And those who disbelieve say, 'Do not listen to this Qur'aan and make noise in the midst of it (being recited) so that you may overcome.'"**[50]

The weakness of Islaam since the Middle ages up to the point where most of its empire disappeared is only so because of the abandonment of the contemplation of the Qur'aan, of reciting it and acting by it."[51]

---

[49] *Miftaa<u>h</u> Daar as-Sa'aadah*, page 204.

[50] Soorah Fu<u>ss</u>ilat (41):26.

[51] *Mukhta<u>s</u>ar Tafseer al-Manaar*, 3/170

Thus, the Noble Qur'aan is one of the greatest fortifiers of *eemaan* and the most beneficial reasons behind its increase.

It increases the *eemaan* of the slave in many diverse ways. Ibn as-Sa'dee says: "It increases it in many ways. Indeed, as for the believer, by simply reciting the *aayaat* of Allaah and becoming acquainted with the truthful information and fine rulings present within it, he attains an abundant goodness from the affairs of *eemaan*. How will it then be if he contemplates on it proficiently and understands its aims and secrets?[52]

However, one must know that the increase of *eemaan* that arises from the recitation of the Qur'aan does not happen unless one concentrates on understanding the Qur'aan, applying it and acting by it. The case is not that he simply reads it without understanding or contemplation, as many people who read the Qur'aan will find it to be their adversary and opponent on the Day of Judgement.

It has been affirmed on the Prophet (ﷺ) that he said: *"Verily, Allaah raises up a people with this Book and He abases others."*[53] It has also been affirmed that he (ﷺ) said: *"...and the Qur'aan is either a proof for you or against you."*[54]

So it is a proof for you and it increases your *eemaan* if you act by it or it is a proof against you and it decreases your *eemaan* if you neglect it and do not observe its boundaries.

Qatadah stated: "Not a single person sits down with this Qur'aan except that he then rises with either some increase or decrease."[55]

Al-Hasan al-Basree says in clarifying the meaning of contemplating the Qur'aan: "...However, by Allaah, it is not by memorising its letters

---

[52] *At-Tawdeeh wa al-Bayaan li Shajarah al-Eemaan*, Page 27.

[53] Related by Muslim, 1/559.

[54] Related by Muslim, 1/203.

[55] Related by Ibn al-Mubaarak in *az-Zuhd*, page 272, al-Aajurree in *Akhlaaq Hamlah al-Qur'aan*, page 73, al-Marwazee in *Qiyaam al-Layl*, Page 77 of the concise version. Al-Baghawee mentioned it in his *Tafseer*, 3/133.

and neglecting its boundaries. To the extent that one of them says, 'I recited the whole Qur'aan and did not miss out a single letter!' and by Allaah, he missed out the whole of the Qur'aan; no Qur'aan is seen in his character or deeds! To the point that one of them says, 'Verily, I can recite a Soorah with a single breath!' By Allaah, these are not reciters or scholars, they are not wise or pious. Whenever the reciters are of this type, may Allaah not increase their like amongst the people!''[56]

May Allaah have mercy upon al-Hasan. I wonder as to what he would say if he witnessed the reciters of our present time? Reciters, who have been infatuated with being melodious, with correctly pronouncing the letters and flowering them, whilst they squander and neglect the limits.

In fact, the ears of the people when listening to the Qur'aan, also turn to the pronunciation of the words and the melody whilst neglecting to hearken or to contemplate on the word of Allaah.

In any case, there is no objection whatsoever to the *tajweed* of the Qur'aan, to recite it slowly and melodiously, and to render it in a fine way. The objection however, is in over-burdening oneself and being obstinate in pronouncing the letters **without** paying any regard or attention to establishing the commands that were the reason for the revelation of the Qur'aan. To the extent that you do not see in many of them the fear brought about by the limits of Allaah, indeed, nor do you see within them application of the Qur'aan in character or deed.

You find a reciter amongst them, who has memorised the Qur'aan and who correctly pronounces the letters, shaving his beard or lengthening his lower garment. In fact, he may neglect performing prayer in its totality or in congregation, and other such sinful acts, to the extent that one of them – and Allaah's help is sought - opened a music party for an immoral woman with *aayaat* of the Noble Qur'aan. He recited as an introduction to her singing, *aayaat* from the Noble Qur'aan!

[56] Related by 'Abdur-Razzaaq in his *Musannaf*, 3/363, Ibn al-Mubaarak in *az-Zuhd*, page 274, al-Aajurree in *Akhlaaq Hamlah al-Qur'aan*, page 41, and al-Marwazee in *Qiyaam al-Layl*, Page 76 of the concise version

The speech of our Lord is too great to be dishonoured by the likes of such. It suffices me to repeat what al-Hasan, may Allaah have mercy upon him, said, 'Whenever the reciters are of this type, may Allaah not increase their like amongst the people!'

Ibn al-'Arabee mentioned, when describing the reciters of his time being preoccupied with reciting the words of the Qur'aan accurately while neglecting its rulings, and taking it up as a profession when the Qur'aan was only revealed to be acted by: "...but when this recitation became a profession, they beautified it and vied with it, spent their life – without any need for them - on it. One of them dies and he was able to raise the Qur'aan in speech as a pot is raised but he broke its meanings as a vessel is broken. Thus, he was not consistent with any of its meanings.[57]

Hence, the Muslim must learn how to derive benefit from the Qur'aan before he begins to recite it in order for its benefit to be achieved. Ibn al-Qayyim, may Allaah have mercy upon him, mentioned in this respect a principle that is of great standing and enormous benefit. It is, "If you want to attain benefit from the Qur'aan, bring your heart together upon reciting or listening to it, and divert your hearing to it, and be present in front of it, in the manner of one who is present and spoken to by the One who spoke it, How perfect He is."[58]

Whoever applies this principle and traverses upon this methodology when reciting the Qur'aan or when listening to it, will succeed with both knowledge and action. His *eemaan* will increase and it will establish itself like towering mountains, and Allaah is the One who is asked to give us the *tawfeeq* towards that and every good.

Furthermore, contemplation and reflection over the *aayaat* of Allaah are of two types: "Contemplation over it to arrive at the intended meaning of the Lord and contemplation over the meanings of what

[57] *Al-'Awaasim min al-Qawaasim* 2/486, within the book *Aaraa' Abee Bakr Ibn al-'Arabee al-Kalaamiyyah* by 'Ammaar at-Taalibee.

[58] *Al-Fawaa'id*, page 5. Also, refer to *al-Fataawa* of Ibn Taymiyyah, 16/48-51 and 7/236-237.

Allaah called His servants to reflect on. The first is contemplation over the Qur'aanic evidence and the second is contemplation over the witnessed evidence. The first is contemplation over His *aayaat* that are heard (i.e., the Qur'aan) and the second is contemplation over His *aayaat* that are witnessed (i.e., the universe and what it contains)."[59] This was stated by Ibn al-Qayyim.

The discussion mentioned here centres on the contemplation of Allaah's *aayaat* that are heard. As for reflection on His *aayaat* that are seen and witnessed, discussion on this will follow shortly by the will of Allaah.

ii. Knowledge of Allaah's Most Beautiful Names and Most Exalted Attributes

The knowledge of the names of Allaah and His attributes that are mentioned in the Book and *Sunnah*, which signify Allaah's absolute perfection from all angles, is one of the greatest branches of knowledge that causes the increase of *eemaan*.

To occupy oneself with learning them, understanding them, and fully investigating them embodies many great benefits, such as:

1. The knowledge of *Tawheed al-Asmaa wa as-Sifaat* is without exception the most noble and glorious of all types of knowledge. Therefore, to engage oneself with understanding it and investigating into it is an engagement of the highest of pursuits and the attainment of such knowledge is of the most noble of gifts (from Allaah).

2. Knowledge of Allaah leads to love of Him, fear and reverence of Him, hope in Him and sincerity of action for Him alone. This is the cornerstone of the servant's happiness. There is no way towards knowing Allaah except by way of knowledge of His names and attributes and to acquire the understanding of their meanings.

[59] *Miftaah Daar as-Sa'aadah*, page 204.

3. Allaah created creation so that they may know and worship Him. This is the purpose that is demanded of them. Thus, to occupy oneself with this is in effect to occupy oneself with that which one was created for. To leave and make waste of this, is none other than a disregard for that which one was created for. It is indeed distasteful of the servant, who never ceases to reap the many bounties of Allaah upon him and whom the favour of Allaah upon him is enormous from every aspect, that he remains ignorant of his Lord and averse to wanting to know Him.

4. One of the articles of *eemaan*, or rather, the most excellent and origin of them all is *eemaan* in Allaah. *Eemaan* is not merely the proclamation of the servant, 'I have *eemaan* in Allaah' without him possessing any knowledge of his Lord. In fact, the reality of *eemaan* is for him to know the One that he has *eemaan* in and to exert ones efforts to knowing His names and attributes until he reaches the level of certainty. The level of the slave's *eemaan* lies in proportion to the knowledge he has of his Lord. The more he knows of his Lord, the more his *eemaan* will increase. Likewise, the less he knows of his Lord, the less his *eemaan* will be. The closest way that will lead him to this is by contemplating over His attributes and names (ﷻ).

5. Knowledge of Allaah (تعالى) is the origin of everything, to the extent that even the one who truly knows Allaah concludes from his knowledge of Allaah's attributes and actions with regard to that which Allaah does and the rulings that He legislates. This is because Allaah only does that which is conformant to the dictates of His names and attributes. His actions centre on justice, favour and wisdom, so the laws that Allaah legislates are only done so in accordance to the dictates of His praise, wisdom, favour and justice. Thus, the information Allaah relates is all true and truthful and His commands and prohibitions are all just and wise.

Amongst these benefits is also the fact that the knowledge of the most beautiful names of Allaah and of His most exalted attributes brings about their effects of servitude and humility. Every attribute has a specific form of servitude connected to it, these are the requisites of this attribute and the requisites of possessing knowledge and correctly understanding the attribute. This covers all forms of worship that are manifested upon the heart and limbs.

To elaborate, the knowledge of the servant that Allaah alone is able to harm and benefit, give and withhold, to create, sustain, to give life and cause death, will produce the worship of *tawakkul* it its inner form (i.e., in the heart) and the requisites and fruits of *tawakkul* in its apparent form (i.e., upon the limbs).

If the servant realises that Allaah hears, sees and knows, and the fact that not a single atom in the heavens and earth escape Him, and that He knows the secret and hidden, and what the treacherous eyes behold and what the breasts conceal, this will make him preserve his tongue, limbs, and the notions of his heart from anything which displeases Allaah. He will make these limbs devoted to what Allaah loves and is pleased with.

If he knows that Allaah is rich, generous, kind, merciful and is enormously benevolent, this will create a strength of optimism, and this optimism will give birth to many types of hidden and apparent servitude, all in proportion to his understanding and knowledge.

Likewise, if he is aware of the perfection and beauty of Allaah, this will grant him a specific love and a great longing to meet Him; this in turn, produces several forms of servitude.

In light of this, one sees that all forms of servitude to Him are related back to the dictates of the names and attributes.[60]

Thus, if the servant knows his Lord in the correct and demanded way, and in the way that is free of the methods of the people who deviated in their understanding of Allaah; such (devaint) methods, which are built upon *tahreef, ta'teel, takyeef* or *tashbeeh* of the names and attributes of Allaah. Whosoever escapes from these false *kalaamiyyah* methodologies, which in effect are the greatest of matters that ob-

[60] Refer to *Miftaah Daar as-Sa'aadah* of Ibn al-Qayyim, pages 424-425. For a similar but more detailed discussion, see *al-Fawaa'id*, also by Ibn al-Qayyim, pages 128-131.

struct the slave's way to knowing his Lord and cause decrease of *eemaan* and its weakness, and instead knows his Lord by His most beautiful names and exalted attributes that He Himself introduced His creation to, which are mentioned in the Book and *Sunnah*, and understands them upon the methodology of the *Salaf as-Saalih*, then he will indeed have been given the *tawfeeq* towards the greatest cause behind the increase of *eemaan*.

A report from the Prophet (ﷺ) has been ascertained, which relates that (a particular set of) ninety-nine names belong to Allaah and as for whosoever enumerates them, this will be a reason for his entry into paradise. Recorded in the *Saheehayn*, is the *hadeeth* of Aboo Hurayrah, may Allaah be pleased with him, in which he says, 'The Messenger of Allaah (ﷺ) said: *"To Allaah belong ninety-name names, one hundred less one, whoever enumerates them will enter Paradise."*[61]

"The meaning of 'enumerate' (here) is not just counting them, as an unrighteous person is able to count them. The meaning is none other than acting by them."[62]

Hence, one must understand the names and attributes as well as know the meanings they impart in order to completely benefit from them.

Aboo 'Umar at-Talamankee states: "From the perfection of the knowledge of Allaah's names and attributes that the supplicant and memoriser is required to know, which the Messenger of Allaah (ﷺ) said is the knowledge of the names and attributes, the benefits they embody and realities they indicate. Whoever does not know of this, is not one who has knowledge of the meanings of the names or who has benefited from the realities they indicate when mentioning them."[63]

Ibn al-Qayyim mentioned three levels of enumerating the names of Allaah:

---

[61] Related by al-Bukhaaree (5/354, 11/214 & 12/377, *al-Fath*) and Muslim 4/2063.

[62] *Fath al-Baari'*, 11/226, this statement was made by al-Aseelee.

[63] *Fath al-Baari'*, 11/226.

- The first level, to memorise their words and number.
- The second level, to understand their meanings and implications.
- The third level, to make *du'aa* (i.e., supplicate) to Allaah with them, this encompasses both supplication of worship and supplication of request.[64]

Ibn Sa'dee says in explanation of the phrase 'enumerates them' found in the aforementioned *hadeeth* of Aboo Hurayrah: "i.e., whoever memorises them, understands their meanings, believes in them and worships Allaah with them, will enter Paradise. Since it is only the believers who will enter Paradise, it becomes apparent that this is the greatest source and constituent towards the attainment of *eemaan* and it's strength and stability. Knowledge of Allaah's names is the foundation of *eemaan* and *eemaan* traces back to it."[65]

Consequently, whoever knows Allaah in this manner will be amongst those who have the strongest of *eemaan*, the most intense in obedience and worship of Allaah, and one who has the greatest fear and awareness of Allaah (سبحانه).

Allaah (تعالى) says:

"It is only those who have knowledge amongst His slaves who fear Allaah. Verily, Allaah is All-Mighty, Oft-Forgiving."[66]

Ibn Jareer at-Tabaree states in his commentary to this aayah: "Allaah, may his mention be exalted, says, 'Those who fear Allaah and shield themselves from His punishment by being obedient to him, are none other than those who have knowledge of His capability over anything that He desires and that He does what He likes.' The reason being that whoever is certain of Allaah's retribution as a consequence of

[64] *Badaa'i' al-Fawaa'id*, 1/164.

[65] *At-Tawdeeh wa al-Bayaan*, page 26.

[66] Soorah Faatir (35):28.

disobedience to Him, he will fear and dread Him for fear of being punished by Him."[67]

Ibn Katheer writes: "i.e., those who truly fear Him as He should be, are none other than the learned, who know Him. The reason being that the more the knowledge of al-'Adheem, al-'Aleem, the One characterised with attributes of perfection and depicted with the most beautiful names is, the greater and more complete is the knowledge of Him, the greater and more will be the fear of Him."[68]

One of the *Salaf* summed up this meaning with a concise expression, he said: "Whoever has more knowledge of Allaah, will have more fear of Him."[69]

Ibn al-Qayyim, may Allaah have mercy upon him, says: "There does not exist a need of the souls that is greater than their need for the knowledge of their Maker and Originator, and for possessing love of Him, mentioning Him, being delighted at Him, and for seeking a means and position with Him. However, there is no route to this except by way of knowledge of His characteristics and names. Thus, the more knowledgeable the slave is of these names and attributes, the more knowledgeable he will be of Allaah, the more will be his quest of Him, and the nearer he will be to Him. Likewise, the more averse he is to the names and attributes, the greater ignorance he will have of Allaah, the more will be his dislike for Him and the further away he will be from Him. **Allaah affords the slave a status with Him that is in accordance with the status that the slave gives to Allaah with himself**..."[*]

Knowledge of Allaah strengthens the area of fear and awareness and gives growth to hope in the heart. It increases the *eemaan* of the servant and yields many types of worship.

[67] *Tafseer at-Tabaree*, 12/132.

[68] *Tafseer Ibn Katheer*, 3/553.

[69] *Ar-Risaalah al-Qushayriyyah* of Aboo al-Qaasim al-Qushayree, page 141. The one who made this statement is Aboo 'Abdullaah Ahmad ibn 'Aasim al-Antaakee, refer to his biography in *As-Siyar*, 11/409.

[*] *Al-Kaafiyah ash-Shaafiyah*, pg 3-4.

The only way and route to this knowledge is via reflecting on the Book of Allaah and on His names, attributes and actions that Allaah has made His servants aware of upon the tongues of His Messengers. It is also by reflecting on those matters that Allaah has declared Himself exalted over, which are neither becoming of him nor befitting to Him (سبحانه).

It is by contemplating over His days and actions towards His *awliyaa* and enemies, which He has informed His servants of and made them bear witness to. This is so that they may use it as evidence to arrive at the fact that He is their True Evident Deity - worship is not befitting to anyone besides Him.

They may also use this as evidence of the fact that Allaah has absolute power over all things; that He is fully aware of everything; that He is severe in retribution, oft forgiving and most merciful; that He is the All Mighty, the All Wise and that He does what He wants. He is the One who comprehends everything with His knowledge and mercy and all of His actions revolve around wisdom, mercy, justice and benefit. Not a single action of His is excluded from this.

Such benefit, can only be derived by way of reflection on His words and by looking at the effects of His actions.[70]

As for the one who opposes this mainstream way, deviates from this path, and traverses the path of those who deviated in understanding Allaah, then how far he is indeed from the knowledge of his Lord and Creator! In fact, he will be the weakest of people who know their Lord and the least of them who have fear and reverence for Him.

Ibn al-Qayyim, may Allaah have mercy upon him, says, after explaining that the reason behind the difference present within people concerning their understanding of Allaah, relates back to the difference present in their knowledge and awareness of the Prophetic texts, in its comprehension, and in the knowledge of the falsity of the misconceptions that oppose the reality of these texts, he says (after this): "...and you will find those who are weakest in understanding to be

[70] See *Miftaah Daar as-Sa'aadah* of Ibn al-Qayyim, page 202.

the people of false censured speech; the speech that the *Salaf* condemned. This traces back to their ignorance of the texts and its meanings and the firm establishment of false misconceptions in their hearts."

He then informs that the masses reside in a better state than them and that they posses a stronger knowledge of their Lord, he says: "...and if you were to contemplate over the state of the masses, who are not believers according to the view of most of them, you will find them having more understanding than them and having stronger *eemaan*, greater submission to the revelation and a higher level of submission to the truth."[71]

Before this, Ibn al-Qayyim, may Allaah have mercy upon him, highlights the importance of having insight and correct understanding of *Tawheed al-Asmaa wa as-Sifaat* and of understanding it upon the methodology of the *Salaf as-Saalih*. He also points out the importance of staying clear of the false misconceptions of the people of *kalaam*, which destroy this *tawheed*.

Thereafter, he mentions concise beneficial words that lead towards this insight and understanding, he says: "The substance of all this is that your heart witnesses the Lord, in ascension above His Throne, speaking with his commands and prohibitions, seeing the movements of the world, its celestial part and earthly part, its figures and its essences; hearing their voices, observant of their consciences and secrets.

The decrees of the kingdoms being under His disposal and order, they descend from Him and rise back up to Him. His angels are at His service; they execute His orders across the regions of His kingdoms.

He is characterised with attributes of perfection and described with qualities of magnificence. He is elevated above defects, deficiencies and having any like. He is as He has described Himself in His Book, and over and above what His creation depicts Him with.

[71] *Madaarij as-Saalikeen*, 1/125.

He is ever living and will not die. He is self-sustaining, supports all and does not sleep. He is fully cognisant; not a single atom in the Heavens or the Earth escapes Him. He is an all-seer; He views the crawling of a black ant upon a massive rock on a pitch-dark night. He is an all-hearer; He hears the cries of the voices with the diversity of languages concerning their multifarious needs.

His words are complete and perfect in truthfulness and justice. His attributes are too majestic to be likened or equated to the attributes of His creation. His essence is highly exalted above any likeness to other essences outright. His creatures are all-embraced by His actions with justice, wisdom, mercy, benevolence and favour.

To Him belong the creation and command. To Him belong all-blessings and favour, the whole dominion and all-praise, and commendation and glory.

He is first, there being nothing before Him and He is last, there being nothing after Him. He is *Dhaahir,*[72] there being nothing above Him and He is *Baatin,*[73] there being nothing closer than Him.

His names are all names entailing commendation, praise and glory; this is why they are termed 'the most beautiful'. His attributes are all attributes of perfection, His characteristics are all characteristics of splendour, and His actions are all wise, merciful, of benefit and just.

Every single creation points to Him and directs one who sees Him with the view of insight, towards him.

He did not create the Heavens, the Earth and that between them without purpose, nor did He leave man neglected and void (of any purpose). Rather, He created creation in order for them to establish *tawheed* of Him and worship of Him.

---

[72] *Dhaahir*: Indicates the greatness of His attributes and the insignificance of every single creation in respect to His greatness and Highness, for He is above all of His creation with regard His essence and attributes. [t]

[73] *Baatin*: Indicates His awareness and knowledge of all secrets, of that which is in the hearts and the most intimate of things just as it indicates His closeness and nearness to all in a manner that befits His majesty. [t]

He showered them with His bounties so that they can employ the expression of gratitude of these bounties to attain even more of His generosity.

He introduced Himself to His servants in many different ways. He explains His signs in various ways and diversified for them the indications.

He called them to love Him from all doors and extended between Himself and them the strongest of means of His covenant.

Hence, He completed His ample favours upon them, established His perfect proof on them, poured His bounties upon them, wrote upon Himself mercy, and insured in His Book, which He wrote, that His mercy overpowers His anger.[74]

Thus, whoever's knowledge of Allaah is of this like and he has understanding of this type of insight, he will be of those who have the strongest *eemaan*, who are the best in augmentation, glorification and observance of Allaah (ﷻ), who are most obedient to Him and who seek nearness to Him the most.

People in this respect are of various levels, some who achieve little and others who achieve much more.

iii. To Look Attentively at the Biography of the Noble Prophet (ﷺ)

For sure, a cause for the increase of *eemaan* is to look into the life story of the Prophet (ﷺ), to study it and to reflect on his fine qualities and noble and praise worthy characteristics that are mentioned in his biography.

He is the one who was trusted by Allaah with His revelation, the chosen one from amongst His creation and His ambassador between

[74] *Madaarij as-Saalikeen*, 1/124-125. Refer to *Madaarij* again, 3/252-253 and *al-Waabil as-Sayyib* of Ibn al-Qayyim, pages 125-129.

Himself and His slaves. He is the one who has been sent with the upright religion and the straight path. Allaah sent him as a mercy unto the worlds, a leader of the righteous and as a proof over all of His creation.

Allaah sent him after a period that was void of any Messengers and guided by him towards the most upright of paths and clearest of ways.

Allaah enjoined upon His slaves obedience of His Prophet, exaltation of him, respect for him, love of him and the establishment of the rights that are due to him.

He sealed the paths that lead to Paradise, for it will not be opened for anyone unless he comes by way of the Prophet (ﷺ).

Allaah opened his breast, raised his mention and removed his burden from him. He decreed subservience and humiliation for the one who opposes his command. In fact, there does not exist a way for anyone who has come after him to attain happiness in this world and the next except by following him, being obedient to him and traversing upon his path.

Ibn al-Qayyim, may Allaah have mercy upon him, said: "...and within this context, you can comprehend that the dire need of the slaves, which surpasses **all other** needs, is the need for knowledge of the Prophet, for that which he brought, for the belief in what he informed of and for having obedience to his commands.

This is because there is no way towards happiness and success in this life and the next other than through the Messengers. There is no way of knowing the good and the bad in detail except by their way. Furthermore, one can definitely not attain the pleasure of Allaah unless it is through them.

Thus, the good of actions, statements, and qualities is none other than their guidance and that which they brought. They are the preponderate scales with which, all actions, statements and qualities are weighed against. By following the Messengers, the people of truth are distinguished from the people of deviation.

Hence, the necessity for them is greater than the necessity of the body for its soul, than the necessity of the eye for its light and the soul for its life.

In all, with regard to any dire need that is supposed, the necessity of the servant for the Messengers will be much greater.

What is your opinion of one whom if you are deprived of his guidance and that which he brought, for even a blink of an eyelid, your heart falls into ruin and it becomes similar to the fish that is void of water and placed in the frying pan? The state of the servant when his heart leaves that which the Messengers brought is like this state, or rather, even worse. However, only the heart that is alive can sense this, for '*a wound inflicted upon a corpse does not feel any pain whatsoever.*'[75]

If the happiness of the slave in both abodes is dependent upon the guidance of the Prophet (ﷺ), it becomes a must upon everyone who sincerely wants to advise his own self and who desires his own salvation and happiness, to know of the guidance, life story of the Prophet (ﷺ) and his standing, which will take him out of the circle of those who are ignorant of him and will place him amongst his followers, his group and party.

People in this respect are an assortment of those who know little, those who know more and those who are deprived of any knowledge whatsoever. All favour is in Allaah's hand, He bestows it to whoever He wills and Allaah is the possessor of great bounty."[76]

This is why one who studies the biography and contemplates over the characteristics and qualities of the Prophet (ﷺ) that are mentioned in the Book, the *Sunnah* and in the books that specifically deal with his life-history, he will inevitably acquire much good for himself.

---

[75] The second part from a line of poetry by al-Mutanabbee. The first part reads: *"Whoever weakens, it becomes easy to disgrace him."* This is from a poem that was said to praise Aboo al-Hasan 'Alee Ibn Ahmad al-Murree. Refer to *Deewan al-Mutanabbee*, pg. 164, published by Daar Beirut.

[76] *Zaad al-Ma'aad*, 1/69-70.

His love for the Prophet (ﷺ) will increase and this love will give rise to adherence to him in speech and action; 'The foundation of all foundations is knowledge, and the most beneficial knowledge is looking into the biography of the Messenger and that of his companions.'[77]

One who contemplates for example, on the statement of Allaah when describing His Prophet (ﷺ):

لَقَدْ جَآءَكُمْ رَسُولٌ مِّنْ أَنفُسِكُمْ عَزِيزٌ
عَلَيْهِ مَا عَنِتُّمْ حَرِيصٌ عَلَيْكُم بِٱلْمُؤْمِنِينَ
رَءُوفٌ رَّحِيمٌ ﴿١٢٨﴾

> **"Verily, there has come unto you a Messenger from amongst yourselves. It grieves him that you should receive any injury or difficulty. He is anxious over you; for the believers, he is full of pity, kind and merciful."**[78]

And his Saying:

وَإِنَّكَ لَعَلَىٰ خُلُقٍ عَظِيمٍ ﴿٤﴾

> **"And verily, you are indeed upon an exalted standard of character"**[79]

And His Saying:

فَبِمَا رَحْمَةٍ مِّنَ
ٱللَّهِ لِنتَ لَهُمْ ۖ وَلَوْ كُنتَ فَظًّا غَلِيظَ ٱلْقَلْبِ لَٱنفَضُّوا۟ مِنْ حَوْلِكَ ۖ

> **"And it was but by the mercy of Allaah that you dealt with them gently. Had you been severe and harsh-hearted, they would have dispersed away from you..."**[80]

Likewise, there are other *aayaat* in addition to these.

---

[77] *Sayd al-Khaatir* of Ibn al-Jawzee, page 66.

[78] Soorah at-Tawbah (9):128.

[79] Soorah al-Qalam (68):4.

[80] Soorah Aal-'Imraan (3):159.

Look into the *Sunnah*, at the reports of the Companions, may Allaah be pleased with them, on the description of the Prophet (ﷺ). Such as the *hadeeth* of 'Aa'ishah, may Allaah be pleased with her, in which she says: "Whenever the Messenger of Allaah (ﷺ) was given a choice between two matters, he would choose the easiest of the two as long as it did not entail any sin. If it was sinful, he would be the furthest removed from such a thing. He never avenged for his own self; only when the sanctuaries of Allaah were violated would he then avenge them for Allaah."[81]

The *hadeeth* of Anas Ibn Maalik, may Allaah be pleased with him, in which he reports: "I served him (ﷺ) for ten years and by Allaah, not once did he ever say to me, '*uff*[82]'. He never said of something I did, 'Why did you do that?' or of something I did not do, 'Why did you not do that?'"[83]

Anas, may Allaah be pleased with him, also said: "He was the most generous person, the most handsome and the bravest of people."[84]

He also said: "The Messenger of Allaah (ﷺ) was the best person in character and manners."[85]

The *hadeeth* of 'Abdullaah Ibn 'Amr, may Allaah be pleased with him; he says: "The Messenger of Allaah (ﷺ) was never indecent (i.e., in speech, action, etc) by nature and nor did he ever purposely adopt such indecency, and he used to say, 'The best of you, is the finest of you in character and manners.'"[86]

The *hadeeth* of Aboo Sa'eed al-Khudree, may Allaah be pleased with him; he said: "The Messenger of Allaah (ﷺ) was shyer than a virgin in

---

[81] Related by al-Bukhaaree, (6/566 *Fath*) and Muslim 4/1813.

[82] A sound made by someone that can be used to express his uneasiness, dissatisfaction, etc. Refer to Ibn al-Atheer's *an-Nihaayah fee Ghareeb al-Hadeeth*. [t]

[83] Related by al-Bukhaaree, (10/456 *Fath*) and Muslim 4/1805.

[84] Related by al-Bukhaaree, (6/95 *Fath*) and Muslim 4/1802.

[85] Related by Muslim 3/1692.

[86] Related by al-Bukhaaree, (10/456 *Fath*) and Muslim 4/1810.

her quarters, and whenever he disliked something, we would notice that from the expression on his face."[87]

Similarly, there are so many other h̲adeeths that would take a period of time to mention.

Thus, whoever contemplates over these will benefit greatly. Furthermore, this is a great matter, which strengthens the love in the heart of a Muslim for his Prophet (ﷺ) and an increase of love for him (ﷺ) is an increase in *eemaan*. It brings about adherence and righteous actions, which in effect are amongst the greatest openings and ways of guidance.

Ibn al-Qayyim, may Allaah have mercy upon him, mentions that being guided has many reasons and various ways, and that this is from Allaah's kindness towards His servants in light of the differences between their intellectual capacities, minds, perception and insight. He mentions that contemplation over the state and qualities of the Prophet (ﷺ) is one of these ways and that it is the reason for guidance of many a people.

He says: "...and some people are guided by their knowledge of his state (ﷺ), of the perfect character, qualities and actions that he was endowed with, and of the fact that the norm of Allaah with regard to one who possesses such qualities and actions is that He will not humiliate and dishonour him.

This he believes because of his knowledge and understanding of Allaah and that He does not degrade one who is of this standing, just as the mother of the believers, Khadeejah, may Allaah be pleased with her, said to the Prophet (ﷺ), 'Receive glad tidings, for by Allaah, Allaah will never humiliate you; you keep the ties of kinship, you speak truthfully, support the unable, aid the weak and assist in areas of truth'[88]..."[89]

---

[87] Related by al-Bukhaaree, (6/566 *Fath*) and Muslim 4/1809.

[88] Related by al-Bukhaaree, (1/33 *Fath*) and Muslim 1/141. This is part of a lengthy h̲adeeth.

[89] *Miftaah̲ Daar as-Sa'aadah*, page 240, also see page 323.

Ibn as-Sa'dee, may Allaah have mercy upon him, says: "From the means that bring about *eemaan* and is one of its causes, is knowledge of the Prophet (ﷺ) and of the lofty mannerisms and perfect qualities he possessed. The one who truly knows him has no doubt in his honesty and in the truthfulness of what he brought of the Book, *Sunnah* and religion of truth. As Allaah (تعالى) says:

أَمْ لَمْ يَعْرِفُوا۟ رَسُولَهُمْ فَهُمْ لَهُۥ مُنكِرُونَ

"Or is it that they do not recognise their Messenger so they then deny him."[90]

i.e., knowledge of him (ﷺ) necessitates an instant acceptance of *eemaan* from the slave who has not yet believed and an increase of *eemaan* from one who has already believed in him.

Allaah (تعالى) says encouraging them to reflect on the circumstances of the Messenger, which invite towards *eemaan*:

قُلْ إِنَّمَآ أَعِظُكُم بِوَٰحِدَةٍ ۖ أَن
تَقُومُوا۟ لِلَّهِ مَثْنَىٰ وَفُرَٰدَىٰ ثُمَّ تَتَفَكَّرُوا۟ ۚ مَا بِصَاحِبِكُم
مِّن جِنَّةٍ ۚ إِنْ هُوَ إِلَّا نَذِيرٌ لَّكُم بَيْنَ يَدَىْ عَذَابٍ شَدِيدٍ ﴿٤٦﴾

"Say, I exhort you with one thing only: that you stand up for Allaah's sake in pairs or alone and you reflect (on the life-history of the Prophet (ﷺ)); your companion has no madness. He is but a warner to you of a severe punishment at hand.'"[91]

Allaah (تعالى) swears by the perfection of this Messenger and his tremendous character and mannerisms, and also that he is the most perfect of creation, when He says:

نٓ ۚ وَٱلْقَلَمِ وَمَا يَسْطُرُونَ ﴿١﴾ مَآ أَنتَ بِنِعْمَةِ رَبِّكَ بِمَجْنُونٍ ﴿٢﴾
وَإِنَّ لَكَ لَأَجْرًا غَيْرَ مَمْنُونٍ ﴿٣﴾ وَإِنَّكَ لَعَلَىٰ خُلُقٍ عَظِيمٍ ﴿٤﴾

---

[90] Soorah al-Mu'minoon (23):69.

[91] Soorah Saba' (34):46.

> **"Noon. By the pen and what they (i.e., the angels) record. You are not, by the grace of your Lord, an insane person. And indeed, for you there will certainly be an endless reward. And verily, you are indeed upon an exalted standard of character."**[92]

Hence, he (ﷺ) is a great inviter to *eemaan* by way of his praiseworthy qualities, beautiful mannerisms, truthful speech and righteous actions. He is the greatest leader and the perfect role model:

لَّقَدْ كَانَ لَكُمْ فِي رَسُولِ ٱللَّهِ أُسْوَةٌ حَسَنَةٌ

> **"You have in the Messenger of Allaah a beautiful example to follow..."**[93]

وَمَآ ءَاتَىٰكُمُ ٱلرَّسُولُ فَخُذُوهُ وَمَا نَهَىٰكُمْ عَنْهُ فَٱنتَهُوا۟

> **"...And whatever the Messenger gives you, then take it and whatever he prohibits you from, then abstain from it..."**[94]

Allaah mentions concerning those endowed with understanding, who are the distinct of mankind, that they say: **"O our Lord, verily, we have heard a caller"**[95] and he is the noble Messenger **"calling towards eemaan"** by his statements, character, deeds, religion and all his circumstances. **"So we have believed"** i.e., professed an *eemaan* that is not open to any doubt..."[96]

Ibn as-Sa'dee then mentions further on: "This is why the person who is just, who does not have any other inclination besides following the truth, upon merely seeing him and listening to his speech, he races to profess *eemaan* in the Prophet (ﷺ) and has no doubt in his message. In fact, many of them, as soon as they set eyes on his gracious face, they know that it is not the face of a liar..."[97]

---

[92] Soorah al-Qalam (68):1-4.

[93] Soorah al-Ahzaab (33):21.

[94] Soorah al-Hashr (59):7.

[95] Soorah Aal-'Imraan (3):193.

[96] See *at-Tawdeeh wa al-Bayaan* of Ibn as-Sa'dee, pg. 32-33.

[97] *At-Tawdeeh wa al-Bayaan*, pages 29-30.

iv. Pondering Over the Merits and Qualities of the Religion of Islaam

Everything within the religion of Islaam is virtuous and good. Its beliefs are the most correct, truthful and beneficial. Its moral code and mannerisms are the most praise worthy and beautiful of all moral etiquette. Its actions and rulings are the finest and most just of all rulings and legislation.

With such significant observation and beautiful reflection over the fine qualities and advantages of this religion, Allaah adorns the *eemaan* in the heart of the servant and he makes it beloved to him. He does this just as He favoured the best of His creation[98] with such, when He said:

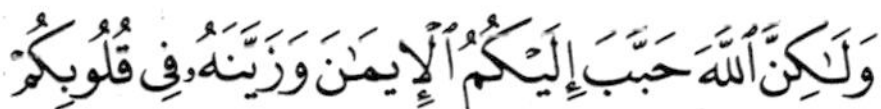

> **"...but Allaah has made *eemaan* beloved to you and has adorned it in your hearts..."**[99]

Thus, *eemaan* in the heart becomes the most cherished and beautiful thing.

Subsequently, the servant tastes the sweetness of *eemaan* and he finds it in his heart. His inner soul then embellishes itself with the foundations and realities of *eemaan* and his limbs adorn themselves with actions of *eemaan*.

Ibn al-Qayyim, may Allaah have mercy upon him, writes: "If you reflect on the overwhelming and dazzling wisdom within this upright religion; this pure path and *sharee'ah* brought by the Prophet Muhammad, of which no expression can contain its perfection, no depiction can grasp its beauty and nothing more superior can be thought up by the minds of the learned even if they were all to be collectively assembled into the mind of the most perfect of them.

---

[98] i.e., the Companions. This is obviously apart from the Prophets and Messengers. [t]

[99] Soorah al-Hujuraat (49):7.

It is enough in itself, that these integral and respectable minds have sensed the beauty of it and bear witness to its excellence and the fact that no other *sharee'ah* that has ever graced the world, is more complete, more sublime and greater. The *Sharee'ah* is itself the witness and the one borne witness to, it is the proof and the one used as proof and it is the claim and the evidence. Furthermore, if the Messenger had not brought any proof for it (i.e., its validity), it itself would be sufficient as proof, as a sign and witness that it is indeed from Allaah."[100]

Consequently, contemplation over the merits and beauties of this religion, looking into the commands, prohibitions, legislation, rulings, moral code and etiquette that it has brought, is one of the greatest motives and incentives for one who does not yet possess *eemaan* in the religion, to embrace it and for the one who already has *eemaan*, to attain an increase in it.

Truly, one who strengthens his contemplation over the fine qualities of this religion and who attains a well-grounded knowledge of it and its beauty and perfection as well as comprehending the ugliness of that which opposes it, will be amongst those who have the strongest *eemaan*, the best of them in steadfastness and stability upon the religion and the most adherent to it.

This is why Ibn al-Qayyim, may Allaah have mercy upon him, says: "The gist here, is that the distinct of this *ummah* and its learned; when their intellects witnessed the beauty of this religion, its magnificence and perfection and when their intellects witnessed the ugliness of that which opposes it, its imperfection and illness, *eemaan* in this religion and love of it became fused with the delight of the hearts.

If one of them were given the choice of either being thrown into the fire or choosing another religion, he would choose to be thrown into the fire and for his limbs to be dismembered rather than choose another religion. These kind amongst the people are those who are

[100] *Miftaah Daar as-Sa'aadah*, page 323, also see page 328 and onwards.

firmly established in *eemaan*, who are the furthest removed from apostasy and those most deserving to remain firm upon the religion until the Day of meeting Allaah."[101]

A *hadeeth* related by Anas Ibn Maalik, may Allaah be pleased with him, gives credit to what Ibn al-Qayyim mentions here. He reports: "The Messenger of Allaah said, '*Three (qualities); whoever possesses them, will find the sweetness of eemaan: that Allaah and His Messenger are beloved to him more than anyone else, that he loves someone only for the sake of Allaah and that he hates to return to kufr just as he hates to be slung into the fire.*'"[102]

Thus, this person who tasted the sweetness of faith; the delight of *eemaan* which has intermingled with the innermost of his heart; whose heart glows with the light of faith and is intensely content with it - will not thereafter return back to *kufr* and deviation, following desires and false beliefs.

Actually, he becomes amongst those who are the most firm in *eemaan*, the most adherent and stable and one who has the strongest attachment to his Lord and Creator.

This is because he embraced Islaam upon knowledge, conviction and understanding. He knew of the beauty of Islaam and its radiance, its splendour, purity and its distinction from all other religions. Hence, he was content with it as a religion and became very intimate to it, so how can he desire a substitute to it, seek to avert himself from it or wish to move on and make a change?

Amongst the benefits derived from this particular *hadeeth* is that it is regarded to be one of the many proofs of the *Ahl as-Sunnah wa al-Jamaa'ah* on the issue of the increase and decrease of *eemaan* and on the different levels of its people. My father, may Allaah protect him, said: "From the *fiqh* of this *hadeeth* and the deductions made from it are..." he then mentioned a number of issues, amongst them that: "within this *hadeeth* is an evidence for the varying levels of people

---

[101] *Miftaah Daar as-Sa'aadah*, pages 340-341.

[102] Related by al-Bukhaaree, (1/60 *Fath*) and Muslim, 1/66.

with respect to *eemaan* and that it increases with obedience and decreases with disobedience because one who possesses all of these three qualities, finds the sweetness of *eemaan* in contrast to one who does not."[103]

v. Reading the Life-Histories of the Salaf of this Ummah

The *Salaf* of this *ummah*: the Companions of the Prophet (ﷺ) and their students and successors in righteousness, people of the first period of Islaam, are the best of all generations. They are the defenders of Islaam, guides for humankind and lions of combat. They are the participants of the great and momentous incidents and events and the bearers and transmitters of this religion to all who came after them. They have the strongest *eemaan* amongst the people, they are the most well grounded in knowledge, have the most pious of hearts and the purest of souls. The specifically chosen amongst them are the Companions of the Prophet (ﷺ), whom Allaah favoured with the sight of His Prophet (ﷺ). He gratified them by granting them sight of his guise and honoured them by allowing them to hear his voice and listen to his speech. They received the religion from him in a fresh and new manner, it took root in their hearts, their souls found tranquillity with it and they remained firm on it on par with the stability of the mountains. It suffices as a representation of their excellence that Allaah addressed them with His saying:

كُنتُمْ خَيْرَ أُمَّةٍ أُخْرِجَتْ لِلنَّاسِ

"You are the best people ever raised up for mankind..."[104]

The meaning of which is, you are the best of all peoples and the most beneficial for the people.

---

[103] *'Ishroon Hadeeth min Saheeh al-Bukhaaree, Diraasatu-Asaaneedihaa wa Sharh Mutoonihaa*, page 168, by my noble father, Shaykh 'Abdul-Muhsin al-'Abbaad.

[104] Soorah Aal-'Imraan (3):110.

In *Saheeh Muslim*, Aboo Hurayrah, may Allaah be pleased with him, reports that the Messenger of Allaah (ﷺ) said: *"The best of my ummah, is the generation that I have been sent in, then those who proceed after them..."*[105]

One who studies the condition of these righteous people, reads their biographies, perceives their sublime qualities and virtues and reflects on what they were upon, such as the tremendous character and mannerisms they had; their adherence to the noble Messenger (ﷺ); their preservation over *eemaan*, fear of sins and disobedience; wariness of *riyaa'* and hypocrisy; their responsiveness to obedience; vying in performance of good deeds; their aversion to this transitory world and dedication to the everlasting Hereafter.

One who does this, will come across during this contemplation and study, a number of fine qualities and numerous characteristics and attributes that attract him towards a truthful impersonation of them and a desire to adorn oneself with their qualities. Mention of them, reminds of Allaah and contemplation over their condition, strengthens *eemaan* and cleanses the heart. Fine indeed, is the verse of poetry:

Relate again their tale to me, O caravan leader
for their tale polishes the very thirsty heart

The areas for the study and reflection on the biographies of these righteous people are the books of *Taareekh* (History), *as-Siyar* (Biographies), *az-Zuhd* (asceticism), *ar-Raqaa'iq* (heart-softening narratives), *al-War'* (piety) and others. One benefits from those of the reports that have been authenticated.

This contemplation and study produces fine imitation of them as Shaykh al-Islaam writes: "Whoever resembles them more, it will be a greater perfection in himself." Furthermore, whoever resembles a people, becomes one of them.

---

[105] Muslim, 4/1964. It is also related in both *Saheehs* by 'Imraan ibn Husayn with the following wording: *'The best of my ummah is my generation, then those who proceed them...'* al-Bukhaaree, (7/3 *Fath*) and Muslim, 4/1964.

All of these aforementioned issues increase *eemaan* and strengthen it. They are issues that are classified under the beneficial knowledge derived from the Book of Allaah and the *Sunnah* of His Messenger (ﷺ) and that which the *Salaf* of this *ummah* were upon.

In addition, branches of knowledge other than religious knowledge like medicine, engineering, astronomy, arithmetic, botany and other branches that people have expanded upon greatly in recent times; branches of knowledge that have been given an attention and concern greater than they deserve, to the point where they have preoccupied many of those connected to it from learning the basic teachings of the religion and matters that are deemed as of necessity to the religion, these branches of knowledge also have a tremendous effect upon the increase of *eemaan* for those who are concerned with and concentrate on acquiring this knowledge, **if** he is sincere in his intention, desires the truth and frees himself from desires.

How many a people have believed and strengthened their *eemaan* as a result of working in medicine and coming across the marvel of Allaah, the perfection of His design of the creation of man and the amazing constituents He assembled him with, which dazzle the minds and bewilder the learned.

Allaah (تعالى) says:

لَقَدْ خَلَقْنَا ٱلْإِنسَٰنَ فِىٓ أَحْسَنِ تَقْوِيمٍ ﴿٤﴾

"We have created man in the best of stature (mould)"[106]

Allaah says:

وَصَوَّرَكُمْ فَأَحْسَنَ صُوَرَكُمْ ۖ وَإِلَيْهِ ٱلْمَصِيرُ ﴿٣﴾

"...and He shaped you and made excellent your shape, and to Him is the final return."[107]

Allaah also says:

[106] Soorah at-Teen (95):4.

[107] Soorah at-Taghaabun (64):3.

"And on the earth are signs for those who have faith with certainty. And also in your own selves, will you not then see?"[108]

Similarly, being occupied with the rest of the branches of knowledge besides medicine also increase the *eemaan* of the person according to his reflection, contemplation and aspiration for the acquisition of the truth. In all, the matter is in the hand of Allaah (سبحانه); He is the one who guides whom He wants to a straight path.

However, these branches of knowledge do not lead to the increase of *eemaan* unless they are accompanied with reflection and contemplation over Allaah's splendid *Aayaat* and His evident proofs. If they are void of this, this grand benefit and tremendous effect will also be rendered void and these branches of knowledge will not benefit one knowing them, in the sense that it returns an increase, strength and stability to his *eemaan*.

This shows us the importance of reflecting and contemplating over Allaah's *Aayaat* and His different creations. This is the second cause for the increase of *eemaan* and is the subject of the next discussion.

2. Reflecting on the Universal Signs (*Aayaat Kawniyyah*) of Allaah

For certain, contemplating over these signs, studying the diverse and amazing creations of Allaah such as the sky, the earth, the sun, the moon, planets and stars, night and day, mountains and trees, rivers and oceans and the many other creations of Allaah that cannot be enumerated, is without doubt one of the greatest causes for *eemaan* and the most beneficial reasons behind its fortification.

Contemplate the creation of the sky, look back up at it time after time. See how it is the greatest sign in its elevation and height, and in its extent and stationariness, whereby it does not climb up like fire or fall descending like a heavy object. It has no pillars and is neither connected from above. Rather, it is held by the might of Allaah.

[108] Soorah adh-Dhaariyaat (51):21-22.

Next, contemplate its evenness and levelness, there is no rift, split or fissure within it. It does not have any curvature or crookedness.

Then consider the colour it has been given, which is the best of colours, the most agreeable to one's sight and that which strengthens it the most.

Ponder on the creation of the earth and at its construction. You will notice that it is one of the greatest signs of its Maker and Originator. Allaah (سبحانه) created it as a resting place and a bed. He made it subservient to His slaves. Allaah placed within it their livelihood and nourishment. He laid down pathways so that they may wander about the land in search for their needs and disposals. He established the earth firmly with mountains, making them pegs, protecting the earth from shaking along with its inhabitants and He expanded its sides and spread it out.

So He extended the earth, spread it out and enlarged it from all its sides. He made it a receptacle for the living, containing them from above as long as they are alive and He made it a receptacle for the dead, containing them from underneath when they die. Thus, its outer is a homeland for the living and its inner is a homeland for the dead.

Thereafter look at it when it is dead, barren and humbled. When Allaah sends down the rains upon it, it stirs and grows. Thus, it rises and turns green and produces every type of lovely growth. It brings forth wondrous vegetation in appearance and sensation, which are delightful to the onlookers and amicable to the feasters.

Next, consider how Allaah has perfected the sides of the earth with mountains that are unshakeable, towering, stern and solid. Consider how He has erected them so perfectly. How he elevated them and made them the most solid parts of the earth, so that they would not dwindle away with the stretch of years and continual succession of rain and wind. Rather, He perfected its creation, fortified its foundation and deposited within them such benefits, metals, minerals and springs, of which He desired.

Now ponder on this delicate and fine air that is held captive between the sky and earth. It is sensed through feeling when blown; its substance is felt and its form cannot be seen.

It runs between the sky and earth and the birds circle and fly in it, swimming with the aid of their wings just as the fish of the sea swim in water. Its sides and ripples collide against each other when in commotion just as the waves of the ocean clash.

Consider how Allaah (سبحانه) forms with this wind, clouds that are held between the sky and earth. The wind excites the clouds causing them to rise and become dense, Allaah then combines them together and merges them. The winds then impregnate it; these winds are those that Allaah named *lawaaqih*, (i.e., impregnators[109]). Allaah then drives it by the wind to the land in need of it.

When it rises and ascends above the land, its water falls upon it. Allaah dispatches the winds whilst the clouds are in the atmosphere; the winds scatter and separate the clouds so that they do not harm or destroy something if the water were to descend upon it in its entirety. Once the land takes its fill and need, the clouds leave off the land and disperse. Thus, these clouds water the earth and are carried by the winds.

Next, consider these oceans surrounding the land regions, which are gulfs of one great sea of water surrounding the whole earth such that even the lands, mountains and cities that are visible, are in relation to the water, like a small island in a massive ocean. The rest of the earth is submerged in water. If the Lord did not hold it with His power and will and if He did not hold back the water, it would overflow onto the lands and rise above it all.

Contemplate on the night and day; they are amongst the most amazing signs of Allaah. See how He made the night for resting and as a covering. It coats the world causing the cessation of activities. Animals retire to their dwellings and the birds to their nests. The souls relax and take rest from the pains of their labour and tiredness until when

[109] Refer to Soorah al-Hijr (15):22 [t].

the souls are reposed and have taken sleep and now look forward to their livelihood and its disposal, the Splitter of the morning (تعالى) brings forward the day, His army giving glad tidings of the morning. It vanquishes that darkness and tears it asunder, unveiling the darkness from the world, thereafter, the inhabitants are able to see. The animals then circulate about the land and proceed to manage their livelihood and welfare and the birds depart from their nests.

What a returning and arising, which is so indicative of the capability of Allaah towards the major return!

Ponder on the condition of the sun and moon when rising and setting to establish the state of night and day. If it were not for the rising of the sun and moon, the affair of this world would become inoperative. How would the people attend to their livelihood and dispose of their affairs whilst the world upon them is dark? How would they take pleasure in their life with the absence of light? So:

تَبَارَكَ ٱلَّذِى جَعَلَ
فِى ٱلسَّمَآءِ بُرُوجًا وَجَعَلَ فِيهَا سِرَٰجًا وَقَمَرًا مُّنِيرًا ﴿٦١﴾ وَهُوَ
ٱلَّذِى جَعَلَ ٱلَّيْلَ وَٱلنَّهَارَ خِلْفَةً لِّمَنْ أَرَادَ أَن يَذَّكَّرَ أَوْ أَرَادَ
شُكُورًا ﴿٦٢﴾

> **"Blessed be He who has placed in the heaven huge stars and has placed therein a great lamp (i.e., the sun) and a moon giving light. He is the one who placed the night and day in succession, for such who desires to remember or desires to show his gratitude."**[110]

Examine the creation of the animals, with all their diverse characteristics, species, forms, usefulness, colours and endowed marvels. Some of them walk upon their bellies, some on two legs and some on four. Some of them have feet as weapons in the form of claws; some have beaks as weapons, like the eagle, vulture and the crow. Others have teeth as weapons and yet others have horns as weapons for use in defence of themselves.

---

[110] Soorah al-Furqaan (25):61-62.

Reflect and take heed in general from the setting of this world, the formation of its parts and the excellence of its arrangement and order, proving most cogently, the perfection of the capability of its Creator and the perfection of His knowledge, wisdom, benevolence and delicateness.

If you do reflect on the world, you will notice it to be like a house that has been built and prepared with all of its apparatus, interests and all that it is in need of.

Thus, the sky is its roof that is hoisted above it. The land is its bed; it is a mat, bedding and an abode for the occupant. The sun and moon are two lamps that shine within it. The stars are lights, an adornment and guide for those who move about along the paths of this house. Gems and minerals are stored within it, like the provisions and storehouses that have been prepared and set; each and every thing of it is for its own specific purpose and use that befits it. All kinds of vegetation have been prepared for the purposes of the house. Varieties of animals have been laid out for its welfare, for mounting; providing milk; nourishment; clothing; enjoyment; employment and keeping guard.

Moreover, the human being has been declared as the king, being commissioned with all of this. He is the one who rules and disposes by his actions and commands.

Within all this, is the greatest sign and strongest proof of the Creator, the All knowing, the Wise and fully cognisant, who has set proper measure and order for his creation in the finest way.

In fact, reflect and take heed in particular, from Allaah's creation of yourself, O person.

Consider the start, middle and end of your creation. Look with all insight at the beginning of your creation, from a trickle of dirty despised fluid; whereby the Lord of all lords extracted this fluid from between the back-bone and ribs, guided it by His might with the narrowness of its channels and the diversity of its passages up until Allaah brings it to its abode and place of assembly.

See how Allaah united the male and female and placed love between them and how He led them with the chain of desire and love to come together, which is the cause behind the synthesis and formation of a child.

Look at how He predestined those two fluids despite the distance apart from each person. He brought them from the depth of veins and organs and gathered them to one place. He prescribed for them a firmly established dwelling. Air cannot get to it to spoil it; cold cannot get to it to harden or congeal it and no accidentals extend to it.

Allaah then transforms that white saturated trickle into a red clinging-like substance (that resembles a leech), which inclines towards a black colour. Allaah then makes it into a chewed lump (of flesh) completely different to the clinging-like substance in its colour, essence and form. Allaah then fashions it into bare bones without any clothing, which is contrary to the chewed lump in form, look, proportion, feel and colour and so on, the stages of a person's creation make a gradual process up until he emerges upon these forms that Allaah has fashioned him with; He originated for him, hearing, sight, a mouth, nose and the rest of the openings. He extended and spread out his legs and arms and separated their ends into fingers and toes and then further split them into phalanxes. He also assembled the inner organs such as the heart, stomach, liver, spleen, lungs, womb, vesica, intestines; each one has a proportion and benefit specific to it, so how perfect is, the One Who created (everything) and then proportioned (each thing appropriately) and Who measured and guided, Who said:

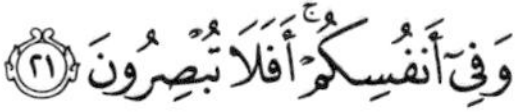

"And also in your own selves, will you not then see?"[111]

"All of creation, from the atom to the Throne, are connected pathways to acquiring knowledge of Allaah (تعالى) and are profound evidences pointing to His eternality. The Universe, in totality, is made up of tongues uttering the oneness of Allaah. The world, in its entirety, is

[111] Soorah adh-Dhaariyaat (51):21.

a book, of which the letters of its particulars are read by the discerning, all according to the level of their insights."[112]

So, reflect on these and other signs, which Allaah has created within the Heavens and earth.

Contemplation, close examination and meditation on these signs yield immense benefits in the strengthening and steadfastness of one's *eemaan*, because he apprehends through these signs, the oneness of his King and Creator and His perfection (ﷻ). Consequently, his love, glorification and veneration of Allaah will increase as will his obedience, submission and humbleness before Him. These are amongst the greatest benefits resulting from this reflection.

Ibn al-Qayyim, may Allaah have mercy upon him, says: "If you consider what Allaah has invited His servants to reflect on in His Book, it will impart you with knowledge of Allaah (ﷻ), of his oneness, His attributes of perfection and qualities of magnificence such as the extensiveness of His capability and knowledge and the perfection of His wisdom, mercy, benevolence, kindness, compassion, justice, pleasure, anger, reward and punishment. Thus, with this (all), He introduced Himself to His servants and encouraged them to reflect on His signs.[113]

Ibn as-Sa'dee, may Allaah have mercy upon him, states: "...and one of the causes and incentives for *eemaan* is reflecting on the universe; on the creation of the heavens and earth and on the diverse types of creation contained within them; to look at the human himself and the attributes he possesses, for this is a strong incentive for *eemaan*.

This is because of the greatness of creation found within these present entities, which points towards the might, capability and greatness of their Creator.

It is also because of the prevalent beauty, order and perfection that baffles the learned, which point to the vastness of Allaah's knowledge

---

[112] See *Dhayl Tabaqaat al-Hanaabilah* of Ibn Rajab, 1/307. This is a saying of 'Uthmaan Ibn Marzooq al-Qurashee.

[113] *Miftaah Daar as-Sa'aadah* of Ibn al-Qayyim, page 204.

and the comprehensiveness of His wisdom and it is also because of the assorted benefits and abundant blessings that cannot be counted and are innumerable, which point to the magnitude of Allaah's mercy, generosity and benevolence.

All of this calls to the glorification of its originator and maker, to gratitude of Him, to becoming attached to His remembrance and having sincerity of religion to Him alone; this is the spirit and secret of *eemaan*.[114]

For this purpose, Allaah, *al-Kareem*, (سبحانه) encourages His servants in His book to contemplate on these signs and indications and He directs them to study and reflect in many places within His Book. This is because of the many advantages for the slaves and the immense returns they attain from it. Allaah (تعالى) says:

إِنَّ فِي خَلْقِ ٱلسَّمَٰوَٰتِ وَٱلْأَرْضِ وَٱخْتِلَٰفِ ٱلَّيْلِ وَٱلنَّهَارِ
وَٱلْفُلْكِ ٱلَّتِي تَجْرِي فِي ٱلْبَحْرِ بِمَا يَنفَعُ ٱلنَّاسَ وَمَآ أَنزَلَ ٱللَّهُ
مِنَ ٱلسَّمَآءِ مِن مَّآءٍ فَأَحْيَا بِهِ ٱلْأَرْضَ بَعْدَ مَوْتِهَا وَبَثَّ فِيهَا
مِن كُلِّ دَآبَّةٍ وَتَصْرِيفِ ٱلرِّيَٰحِ وَٱلسَّحَابِ ٱلْمُسَخَّرِ
بَيْنَ ٱلسَّمَآءِ وَٱلْأَرْضِ لَءَايَٰتٍ لِّقَوْمٍ يَعْقِلُونَ ﴿١٦٤﴾

"Verily, in the creation of the heavens and the earth, and in the alternation of night and day, and the ships that sail through the sea with that which is of use to mankind, and the water which Allaah sends down from the sky and makes the earth alive therewith after its death, and the moving (living) creatures of all kinds that he has scattered therein, and in the veering of winds and clouds which are held between the sky and the earth, are indeed signs for people of understanding."[115]

---

[114] *At-Tawdeeh wa al-Bayaan*, page 31. See *ar-Riyaad an-Naadhirah* also by Shaykh as-Sa'dee, pages 258-280.

[115] Soorah al-Baqarah (2):164.

Allaah (تعالى) says:

وَمِنْ ءَايَٰتِهِۦٓ أَنْ خَلَقَكُم مِّن تُرَابٍ ثُمَّ إِذَآ أَنتُم بَشَرٌ تَنتَشِرُونَ ﴿٢٠﴾

"And among His signs is that He created you from dust and behold, you are human beings, becoming wide-spread."[116]

Allaah (تعالى) says:

وَمِنْ ءَايَٰتِهِۦ خَلْقُ ٱلسَّمَٰوَٰتِ وَٱلْأَرْضِ وَمَا بَثَّ فِيهِمَا مِن دَآبَّةٍ وَهُوَ عَلَىٰ جَمْعِهِمْ إِذَا يَشَآءُ قَدِيرٌ ﴿٢٩﴾

"And among His signs is the creation of the heavens and earth, and of all the creatures He has dispersed within them. And He is ever-potent over assembling them all if He so desires."[117]

Allaah (تعالى) also says:

أَفَلَا يَنظُرُونَ إِلَى ٱلْإِبِلِ كَيْفَ خُلِقَتْ ﴿١٧﴾ وَإِلَى ٱلسَّمَآءِ كَيْفَ رُفِعَتْ ﴿١٨﴾ وَإِلَى ٱلْجِبَالِ كَيْفَ نُصِبَتْ ﴿١٩﴾ وَإِلَى ٱلْأَرْضِ كَيْفَ سُطِحَتْ ﴿٢٠﴾

"Do they not look at the camels: how they have been created? And at the heaven: how it is raised? And at the mountains: how they have been rooted and firmly fixed? And at the earth: how it has been spread out?"[118]

There are other numerous similar *aayaat* in the Qur'aan, in which Allaah calls His servants to look at His signs and manifestations of his actions that represent the most supreme evidence of His oneness and singularity and for His might, will and knowledge (ﷻ). It is also

---

[116] Soorah ar-Room (30):20.

[117] Soorah ash-Shooraa (42):29.

[118] Soorah al-Ghaashiyah (88):17-20.

evidence of His benevolence, gentleness and generosity. This is the greatest invitation of His servants towards having love of Allaah, thanking Him, glorifying Him, obeying Him and being attached to His remembrance.

In conclusion, it becomes evident that study and contemplation of the Universe remains as one of the greatest causes of *eemaan* and the most beneficial incentives for it.

3. Exerting Efforts Towards Accomplishing Sincere Righteous Actions

Another cause for the increase and strengthening of *eemaan* is for the Muslim to exert efforts towards enacting sincere righteous actions for the countenance of Allaah (تعالى); he should try to do more (good) deeds and to do them on a regular basis.

This is because for every action that Allaah has legislated, which the Muslim undertakes and with which he makes his intention behind it sincere, it increases him in *eemaan*, since *eemaan* increases because of obedience and ample acts of worship.

Furthermore, the servitude that Allaah has enjoined on His slaves and demanded them to enact, the obligatory and voluntary of them, are distributed among the heart, the tongue and the limbs. Each of them has a servitude specific to it.

Examples of the servitude of the heart that are specific to it are sincerity, love, *tawakkul*, *inaabah*, hope, fear, reverence, awe, contentment, patience and other actions of the heart.

Examples of servitude of the tongue that are specific to it are reading the Qur'aan, *takbeer*, *tasbeeh*, *tahleel*, seeking forgiveness, praising and commending Allaah, sending *salaah* and *salaam* upon His Messenger and other actions that can only be done by the tongue.

As for the servitude of the limbs that are specific to it, examples of this are *sadaqah*, *hajj*, prayer, ablution, proceeding towards the mosque and other such actions that are only possible with the use of the limbs.

Thus, these actions of the heart as well as those of the tongue and the limbs are all from *eemaan* and are inherently present within the true meaning of the word *eemaan*. To perform such actions and to increase in them will therefore result in an increase of *eemaan* and to neglect them and to lessen the performance of them will result in a deficiency of *eemaan*.

i. Actions of the Heart

In reality, actions of the heart are the foundation of the religion. They are its uppermost part and the most important of ordinances. In fact, apparent[119] actions are not accepted if they are void of any actions of the heart; the reason being that the acceptance of all actions are stipulated by sincerity to Allaah (عزّ وجلّ) and sincerity is an action of the heart.

This is why actions of the heart are mandatory upon everyone and the abandonment of such actions can never be deemed praiseworthy under any condition whatsoever.

People are of three levels with regard to the accomplishment of these actions, similar to the case with actions of the body: one who oppresses his own self, one who suffices with that which is obligatory and one who chases after the good.

Consequently, it is imperative of every Muslim that he starts with the purification and rectification of his heart and with having concern for it, before he concentrates with the rectification of his exterior, as no consideration is given to the rectification of the outer whilst the inner is corrupt.

In addition, when the Muslim does rectify his heart with purifying actions, sincerity, truthfulness and love for Allaah (تعالى) and His Messenger (ﷺ), his limbs will turn upright as in the *hadeeth* of an-Nu'maan Ibn Basheer that is recorded in the two *Saheehs*. He said: "I heard the

[119] i.e., actions of the limbs and tongue, which are sensed. [t]

Messenger of Allaah (ﷺ) say: '*...Indeed, and within the body is a morsel of flesh; if it is sound, then the whole body will be sound and if it is corrupt, then the whole body will be corrupt. Indeed, it is the heart.*''[120]

This *hadeeth* contains the greatest indication that the rectification of the slave's outer movements is directly connected to the rectification of the activity of his heart and innersoul.

If his heart is pure, there being only love of Allaah, love of that which Allaah loves, fear of Him and of falling into that which He hates, the movements of his limbs will all become sound. This is in sharp contrast to a corrupt heart which is conquered by a love for desires, chasing lusts and placing the wants of the self first. Whoever is in such a predicament, the movements of his limbs will all be corrupt.

For this reason, it is said that the heart is the king of the limbs and that the rest of the limbs are its soldiers. In addition to this, the limbs are an obedient army to the heart; they race to its obedience and towards the execution of its commands, not opposing it in any matter whatsoever. Thus, if the king is righteous, this army will be a righteous one. If on the other hand, the king is corrupt, the army will, because of this resemblance, also be corrupt.

Only the heart that is pure is of benefit before Allaah, as Allaah (تعالى) says:

يَوْمَ لَا يَنفَعُ مَالٌ وَلَا بَنُونَ ﴿٨٨﴾ إِلَّا مَنْ أَتَى ٱللَّهَ بِقَلْبٍ سَلِيمٍ ﴿٨٩﴾

"The Day whereon neither wealth nor sons will avail, except for the one who comes to Allaah with a pure heart."[121]

The pure heart is the one that is free of all diseases, blights and distasteful matters. It is the heart that contains nothing but love of Allaah, fear of Him and fear of anything that will distance him from Allaah.[122]

[120] Al-Bukhaaree, (1/127 *Fath*) and Muslim, 3/1220.

[121] Soorah ash-Shu'araa' (26):88-89.

[122] See *Jaami' al-'Uloom wa al-Hikam* of Ibn Rajab, page 71.

Shaykh al-Islaam says: "Moreover, the heart is the foundation. If it embodies knowledge and intention, this will take effect on the body without fail. It is not possible for the body to play truant to what the heart desires… so if the heart is righteous as a result of its knowledge and action on *eemaan*, this absolutely necessitates the rectification of the body in apparent speech and action in accordance with complete *eemaan*."*

Consequently, for one to endeavour to fully fight his self in rectifying his heart and to fill it with love of Allaah (ﷻ) and of statements and actions that Allaah loves, is one of the most formidable ways in which one increases his outer and inner *eemaan*.

Ibn Rajab says: "…the heart cannot be rectified unless there settles within it knowledge of Allaah, His greatness, love of Him, fear and awe of Him, hope and *tawakkul* in Him and for it to be overflowing with this. This is the reality of *tawheed* and the meaning of 'none has the right to be worshipped except Allaah.'

So there can be no question for the rectification of the hearts until its deity, which it worships, knows, loves and fears is one deity, having no partner. If there were in the heavens and the earth a deity being worshipped other than Allaah, the heavens and earth would as a result become corrupt, as Allaah (تعالى) says:

"Had there been therein (i.e., the heavens and earth) deities besides Allaah, then for sure both would have been ruined…"[123]

One concludes from this that righteousness cannot be attained by the celestial and earthly worlds until the activity of its inhabitants are made all for Allaah. The movement of the body is dependent on the activity of the heart and its intention. If therefore, the heart's movement and desire are for Allaah alone, it will become sound and all the

---

Al-Fataawaa, 7/187.

[123] Soorah al-Anbiyaa' (21):22.

movements of the body will become sound. If, however, the movement and intent of the heart are for other than Allaah, it will become corrupt and the activity of the body will also become corrupt in accordance to the (level of) corruption within the activity of the heart."[124]

It has been authenticated on the Prophet (ﷺ) that he said: "*Whoever loves for Allaah, hates for Allaah, gives for Allaah and withholds for Allaah has indeed perfected eemaan.*"[125]

'The meaning of this is that with all the motions of the heart and limbs, if they are all for Allaah, the *eemaan* of the servant, both the interior and exterior, will be complete and the goodness of the activity of the heart necessitate goodness of the activity of the limbs.

Thus, if the heart is good, there being only desire of Allaah and of that which He desires, the limbs will only proceed towards that which Allaah desires. Consequently, the limbs hasten towards that which incurs the pleasure of Allaah, they refrain from what Allaah dislikes or what is feared that would be disliked by Allaah even if it is not sure of that.'[126]

Whenever the hearts become righteous with *eemaan*, truthfulness, sincerity and love and no desire for other than Allaah is left in the heart, all the limbs will attain righteousness and they will not move except for Allaah (ﷻ) and only in areas that His pleasure will be attained.

Furthermore, the heart is always occupied in thought, either about its essential afterlife and its betterment, or about the welfare of its worldly life and living, or its thoughts centre on misgivings, false aspirations and hypothetical circumstances.

---

[124] *Jaami' al-'Uloom wa al-Hikam*, page 71. See *al-Waabil as-Sayyib* of Ibn al-Qayyim, page 12.

[125] Related by Aboo Daawood, 4/220, at-Tabaraanee in *al-Kabeer*, number 7737, Ibn Battah in *al-Ibaanah*, 2/658 and others. Al-Albaanee declared it saheeh, see *as-Silsilah as-Saheehah*, 1/658.

[126] *Jaami' al-'Uloom wa al-Hikam*, page 72.

The sum and substance of the rectification of the heart is that you occupy it with thoughts on that which constitute its welfare and true and actual success.

Hence, in the area of knowledge and conceptions, one occupies it with knowledge of what binds one of *tawheed* and its rights, of death and what leads on from it up until entering Paradise and Hellfire and of the ill actions and the ways to protect oneself from committing them. In the area of intentions and resolutions, one occupies it with desires of that which will cause one benefit and to reject desires that which will bring harm upon him.[127]

Indeed, of immense assistance to the servant in this regard is to increase the beneficial observations, which are enacted in the heart, so that his attachment with Allaah strengthens, as the existence of righteous actions is associated to the establishment and great number of these observations in the heart.

Ibn al-Qayyim, may Allaah have mercy upon him, said: "We will by the aid and *tawfeeq* granted by Allaah, point out these observations in a manner that will make known the reality of this matter:

The first observation of the traveller to Allaah and the home of the hereafter, is that there exists in his heart an observation of this world and its insignificance, its trivial fulfilment, extensive futility, vile participants and rapid demise... Thus, if the servant undertakes this observation of the world, his heart will migrate from this world and it will travel to seek the home of the hereafter.

At this moment, an observation of the hereafter and its continuity is enacted in his heart. That it is in all truth, **the real life**. Its inhabitants will never migrate or depart from it. Rather, it is the place of settling, the last stopping point of all travellers and the end of the journey...

Thereafter, an observation of the Fire is made in his heart, of its combustion, blaze and the depth of its pit; its intense heat and the immense torment of its inhabitants. He observes them as they are

[127] See *al-Fawaa'id* of Ibn al-Qayyim, page 310 and 311.

brought forth to it with blackened faces, blue eyed with iron chains and fetters around their necks. When they reach the fire, its doors will be opened in front of their faces and they will witness that abominable sight, whereupon their hearts will be become severed out of regret and sorrow...

Consequently, if this observation is accomplished in the heart of the servant, he will be stripped of sins, disobedience and of following desires and will instead don the guise of fear and caution... How distant he will actually be from disobedience and violations is dependent on the strength of this observation.

This observation will melt away, roast through and expel the destructive remnants and elements within his heart and thereupon, the heart will find the sweetness of well being and its pleasure.

Thereafter, an observation of Paradise is established in the heart and of what Allaah has prepared in it for its inhabitants: things that no eye has ever seen, no ear has ever heard and no imagination of has ever been made within the heart of a person. This is besides the detailed types of bliss Allaah has portrayed to His servants upon the tongue of His Messenger, guaranteeing the loftiest types of pleasure concerning foods, drink, clothes, palaces, delight and happiness. So, enacted in his heart is an observation of an abode, within which Allaah has placed everlasting bliss in its entirety.

Its ground is musk and its pebbles are pearls. Its structure is made up of bricks of gold and silver and of pearly embroidery. Its drink is sweeter than honey, possesses a fragrance more pleasant than musk, is cooler than camphor and tastier than ginger. In relation to its women, if the face of one of them were to be revealed to this world, it would overpower the radiance of the sun. The clothes of the inhabitants are made of the silk of sarsenet and brocades. Their servants are youths looking like scattered pearls. Their fruit will be everlasting, whose season is not limited and supply not cut off. Therein are thrones raised high. Their food is the flesh of the fowls they desire. They will have drink of wine, there being no harmful effect within it and they will not suffer intoxication. Their vegetation is the fruit that they desire. Their view will be of fair females possessing wide lovely eyes like preserved pearls. They will be reclining upon thrones and in that Garden being made happy. In it are what the souls covet, what gratifies the eyes and they will abide in it forever.

If one adds to this observation, the observation of the day of *Mazeed:*[128] looking at the face of the Lord (عزّ وجلّ) and listening to His speech without an intermediary... If this observation is attached to the ones before it, there and then, will the heart race towards its Lord faster than the procession of the wind moving in its direction and the heart will not on its way bother to glance, neither left nor right..."[129]

Hence, if such observations are manifested in the heart of the servant and he contemplates over them, it will be of great help towards the purification of his heart and its eradication of denounced characteristics and ignoble desires and towards the evacuation of any attachment to other than Allaah (سبحانه). Furthermore, it will be a great motive for worship, love, fear, repentance and of feeling in need of Allaah (تعالى).

The intent here is to highlight that one of the greatest incentives for *eemaan*, one of its most beneficial consolidators and most important reasons for its increase and development is the rectification of the

---

[128] i.e., the day of increase. Allaah says in the Qur'aan: لِّلَّذِينَ أَحْسَنُوا الْحُسْنَىٰ وَزِيَادَةٌ **"For those who do righteousness is *al-Husnaa* and more..."** [Soorah Yoonus (10):26]

Allaah also says: لَهُم مَّا يَشَاءُونَ فِيهَا وَلَدَيْنَا مَزِيدٌ **"There (i.e., *Jannah*), they will have all that they desire, and We have *more*"** [Soorah Qaaf (50):35]

Husnaa has been explained to mean *Jannah* and '*more*' to mean seeing Allaah (تعالى).

This is attested to by the *hadeeth* recorded in *Saheeh Muslim* and *Sunan at-Tirmidhee* and related by Suhayb ar-Roomee, may Allaah be pleased with him, in which the Prophet (ﷺ) said: "*When the people of Jannah enter Jannah, Allaah will say, 'Would you like something I can increase you with? They will reply, 'Have you not whitened our faces? Have you not admitted us into Jannah and saved us from the Fire?'*' The Prophet then said: "*Then the veil will be lifted and they will not have been given anything more beloved to them than seeing their Lord.*" In a similar narration, the end reads: "*The Prophet (ﷺ) then recited this aayah:* لِّلَّذِينَ أَحْسَنُوا الْحُسْنَىٰ وَزِيَادَةٌ **"For those who do righteousness is *al-Husnaa* and more..."** [t]

[129] *Madaarij as-Saalikeen*, 3/250-252.

heart through *eemaan*, love of Allaah, His Messenger, of that which Allaah and His Messenger (ﷺ) love and to purify it from anything that opposes or nullifies this.

Allaah is the one who grants *tawfeeq*.

ii. Actions of the Tongue

As for actions of the tongue like the remembrance of Allaah (ﷻ), praising and commending Him, reading His Book, sending *salaah* and *salaam* upon His Messenger (ﷺ), ordering the good, forbidding the evil, *tasbeeh*, seeking forgiveness, supplication and other actions that are performed by use of the tongue, without doubt, performing such actions, on a regular basis and often is one of the greatest causes for the increase of *eemaan*.

Shaykh Ibn as-Sa'dee, may Allaah have mercy upon him, says: "One of the causes that procures *eemaan* is to greaten the remembrance of Allaah at all times and to also supplicate much, which is the core of worship.

Remembrance of Allaah implants the tree of *eemaan* in the heart. It nourishes and develops it. The more the servant increases in his remembrance of Allaah, the stronger his *eemaan* will become.

Just as *eemaan* calls to much remembrance, whoever loves Allaah will mention Him much.[130] Indeed, love of Allaah is *eemaan*, or rather, it is its spirit."[131]

Ibn al-Qayyim mentions in his book *al-Waabil as-Sayyib* that remembrance has a hundred benefits. He listed seventy-three of these benefits,[132] such as that remembrance repels *Shaytaan*. It pleases the Most Beneficent, causes depression and anxiety to disappear and brings joy and happiness. It strengthens the heart and body, illuminates the face

---

[130] As the saying goes: "Whoever loves something, increases in his mention of it." [t]

[131] *At-Tawdeeh wa al-Bayaan*, pg. 32.

[132] See *al-Waabil as-Sayyib*, pg. 84 and onwards.

and heart, brings about sustenance and many other tremendous benefits that he mentioned, may Allaah have mercy upon him, which are attained because of the remembrance of Allaah (عَزَّوَجَلَّ).

Undoubtedly, the greatest and most beneficial benefit in the remembrance of Allaah is the fact that it increases *eemaan,* strengthens it and stabilises it. Accordingly, a number of texts are related in the Book and *Sunnah,* which command and encourage the remembrance of Allaah. They beckon for its increase and show its excellence and importance. Allaah (تعالى) says:

وَاذْكُرُوا اللَّهَ كَثِيرًا لَّعَلَّكُمْ تُفْلِحُونَ

> **"...and remember Allaah much so that you may succeed."**[133]

Allaah (تعالى) says:

وَالذَّاكِرِينَ اللَّهَ كَثِيرًا
وَالذَّاكِرَاتِ أَعَدَّ اللَّهُ لَهُم مَّغْفِرَةً وَأَجْرًا عَظِيمًا ﴿٣٥﴾

> **"...and (for) men and women who remember Allaah much, Allaah has prepared for them forgiveness and a great reward."**[134]

Allaah (تعالى) says:

إِنَّمَا الْمُؤْمِنُونَ الَّذِينَ إِذَا ذُكِرَ اللَّهُ وَجِلَتْ قُلُوبُهُمْ

> **"Indeed, the believers are none other than those whom when Allaah is mentioned, their hearts tremble with fear..."**[135]

Allaah (تعالى) says:

أَلَا بِذِكْرِ اللَّهِ تَطْمَئِنُّ الْقُلُوبُ ﴿٢٨﴾

---

[133] Soorah al-Jumu'ah (62):10.

[134] Soorah al-Ahzaab (33):35.

[135] Soorah al-Anfaal (8):2.

> **"...Verily, it is in the remembrance of Allaah that the hearts (truly) attain tranquillity."**[136]

As recorded in Saheeh *Muslim*, Aboo Hurayrah, may Allaah be pleased with him, reports: "The Messenger of Allaah (ﷺ) was on his way to Makkah when he passed by a mountain known as Jumdaan. He said, *'Travel through, this is Jumdaan: the mufarridoon have excelled.'* Someone asked, 'Who are the *mufarridoon* O Messenger of Allaah?' He replied, *'Men and women who remember Allaah much.'*"[137]

Aboo Dardaa', may Allaah be pleased with him, relates the Prophet (ﷺ) saying: *"Should I not inform you of the best of your deeds, the most sanctifying of them before your Lord and which does more to raise your status with Him. (A deed,) that is better for you than the disbursement of gold and money, or battle with the enemy whereby you strike at their necks and they strike at yours?"* They said: "What is it O Messenger of Allaah?" He replied: *"Remembrance of Allaah."*[138]

'Abdullaah Ibn Busr mentioned that a man said to the Prophet (ﷺ): "O Messenger of Allaah, the rites of *eemaan* are much for me, so tell me of something that I might hold fast to." He answered: *'Let not your tongue cease from the remembrance of Allaah.'*[139]

---

[136] Soorah ar-Ra'd (13):28.

[137] Muslim, 4/2062.

[138] Related by Ahmad, 5/195; Ibn Maajah, 2/1245; at-Tirmidhee, 5/459; at-Tabaraanee in *ad-Du'aa'*, 3/1636; al-Haakim, 1/496; Aboo Nu'aym in *al-Hilyah*, 2/12; al-Baghawee in *Sharh as-Sunnah*, 5/10 and al-Mundhiree mentioned it in *at-Targheeb wa at-Tarheeb*, 2/395 via many chains from Ziyaad Ibn Abee Ziyaad from Abee Bahriyyah from Aboo Dardaa' from the Prophet (ﷺ). Al-Haakim declared: "This *hadeeth* has a chain of narration that is saheeh and it has not been related by al-Bukhaaree or Muslim." Adh-Dhahabee agreed. Ibn 'Abdil-Barr states: "This is related with a connection to the Prophet (ﷺ) via chains that are good." Al-Baghawee and al-Mundharee declared its chain of narration to be *hasan*.

[139] Related by Ibn Abee Shaybah, 10/301 & 13/458; at-Tirmidhee, 5/458; Ibn Maajah, 2/1246 and al-Haakim, 1/495. At-Tirmidhee declared: "The *hadeeth* is *hasan ghareeb*." Al-Haakim said: "This *hadeeth* has a chain of narration that is saheeh and it has not been related by al-Bukhaaree or Muslim." Adh-Dhahabee agreed. Al-Albaanee mentioned in his checking of *al-Kalim at-Tayyib*, page 25: "Its chain of narration is saheeh."

Recorded in the *Saheehayn* is the *hadeeth* of Aboo Hurayrah, may Allaah be pleased with him, in which he reports the Messenger of Allaah (ﷺ) as saying: *"Allaah (تعالى) says, 'Indeed I am as My servant presumes Me to be and I am with him when he remembers Me. So if he remembers Me to himself, I remember him to Myself and if he remembers Me amongst a company, I remember him amongst a company that is better than them...'"*[140] Many other texts are likewise indicative of the excellence and importance of remembrance and of the virtue of engaging in it.

Consequently, if a person turns away from all of this and does not engage his tongue with remembrance of Allaah (عز وجل), his tongue will be engrossed with matters besides it such as backbiting, slander, mockery, lies and obscene language. This is because the slave cannot but speak. Thus, if he does not speak with the remembrance of Allaah (تعالى) and of His commands, he will speak of these things.

Ibn al-Qayyim says: "For the tongue does not keep quiet at all. It is either a tongue that remembers or a tongue that is frivolous and it has to be one of these two.

It is the (nature of the) soul; if you do not preoccupy it with truth, it will occupy you with falsehood. It is the (nature of the) heart; if you do not accommodate it with love of Allaah, it will dwell with love of creation and this is a certain reality. It is the (nature of the) tongue, if you do not preoccupy it with remembrance, it will most definitely occupy you with frivolity.

Thus, choose for your own self one of the two courses and confer upon it one of the two standings."[141]

---

[140] Al-Bukhaaree, (13/384 with *Fath*) and Muslim, 4/2061.

[141] *Al-Waabil as-Sayyib*, pages 166-167 and also see page 87.

ii. Actions of the Limbs

As for the actions of the heart like prayer, fasting, *hajj*, *sadaqah*, *jihaad* and other acts of obedience, they are also reasons for the increase of *eemaan*.

To exert efforts therefore, towards enacting acts of obedience, which Allaah has made incumbent upon His slaves and performing acts that achieve nearness (to Allaah), which Allaah has recommended His servants to undertake and to accomplish these acts in a proficient and complete manner, is one of the most tremendous causes behind the strengthening and increase of *eemaan*.

Allaah (تعالى) says:

قَدْ أَفْلَحَ ٱلْمُؤْمِنُونَ ﴿١﴾ ٱلَّذِينَ هُمْ فِى صَلَاتِهِمْ خَٰشِعُونَ ﴿٢﴾
وَٱلَّذِينَ هُمْ عَنِ ٱللَّغْوِ مُعْرِضُونَ ﴿٣﴾ وَٱلَّذِينَ هُمْ لِلزَّكَوٰةِ
فَٰعِلُونَ ﴿٤﴾ وَٱلَّذِينَ هُمْ لِفُرُوجِهِمْ حَٰفِظُونَ ﴿٥﴾ إِلَّا عَلَىٰٓ
أَزْوَٰجِهِمْ أَوْ مَا مَلَكَتْ أَيْمَٰنُهُمْ فَإِنَّهُمْ غَيْرُ مَلُومِينَ ﴿٦﴾
فَمَنِ ٱبْتَغَىٰ وَرَآءَ ذَٰلِكَ فَأُو۟لَٰٓئِكَ هُمُ ٱلْعَادُونَ ﴿٧﴾ وَٱلَّذِينَ هُمْ
لِأَمَٰنَٰتِهِمْ وَعَهْدِهِمْ رَٰعُونَ ﴿٨﴾ وَٱلَّذِينَ هُمْ عَلَىٰ صَلَوَٰتِهِمْ
يُحَافِظُونَ ﴿٩﴾ أُو۟لَٰٓئِكَ هُمُ ٱلْوَٰرِثُونَ ﴿١٠﴾ ٱلَّذِينَ يَرِثُونَ
ٱلْفِرْدَوْسَ هُمْ فِيهَا خَٰلِدُونَ ﴿١١﴾

"Successful indeed are the believers: those who offer their prayers with all solemnity and full submissiveness; who turn away from *al-Laghw*; who pay the *zakaah*; who guard their chastity, except from their wives or those that their right hands possess, for them, they are free from blame. However, whoever seeks beyond that, then they are the transgressors; those who are faithfully true to their *amaanaat* and covenants and those who strictly guard their prayers. These are indeed the inheritors, who shall inherit *Firdaws*. They shall abide therein forever."[142]

[142] Soorah al-Mu'minoon (23):1-11.

These precious qualities, each one of them profits and develops *eemaan*. They are also characteristics of *eemaan* and fall under its explanation.

So, the attendance of the heart in prayer and the event of the praying person striving with his self to call to mind and heart what he is saying and doing, such as recitation, remembrance, supplication, standing, sitting, bowing and prostration, are reasons for the increase and development of *eemaan*.

Allaah named prayer '*eemaan*' when He said:

وَمَا كَانَ ٱللَّهُ لِيُضِيعَ إِيمَٰنَكُمْ

> **"...and Allaah would never cause your *eemaan*[143] to be lost..."[144]**

Furthermore, concerning the statement of Allaah:

وَأَقِمِ ٱلصَّلَوٰةَ إِنَّ ٱلصَّلَوٰةَ تَنْهَىٰ عَنِ ٱلْفَحْشَآءِ وَٱلْمُنكَرِ وَلَذِكْرُ ٱللَّهِ أَكْبَرُ

> **"...and establish the prayer. Verily, the prayer prevents from all obscenities and evil deeds. And the remembrance of Allaah is greater..."[145]**

Prayer is the greatest obstructer of every obscene and evil deed that negates *eemaan*. In addition, prayer also embodies the remembrance of Allaah, which nourishes and develops *eemaan* because of His saying:

وَلَذِكْرُ ٱللَّهِ أَكْبَرُ

"...And the remembrance of Allaah is greater..."

Likewise, *zakaah* also nurtures and increases *eemaan*, (both) the obligatory type of *zakaah* and its recommended type, as the Prophet

[143] i.e., the prayers that were performed towards the direction of Jerusalem, before the commandment of changing the *qiblah* to the Ka'bah in Makkah. [t]

[144] Soorah al-Baqarah (2):143.

[145] Soorah al-'Ankaboot (29):45.

(ﷺ) has said, "...*and sadaqah is proof.*" i.e., a proof for the *eemaan* of its giver. Hence, it is evidence of *eemaan* and it nourishes and develops it.

Further, to avert from *al-Laghw*, which is any speech or action that is void of good. Instead they (i.e., the believers) speak and do well, and abandon evil in both speech and action. This is without doubt, from *eemaan* and *eemaan* increases and profits from it.

This is why whenever the Companions, may Allaah be pleased with them, and those after them sensed heedlessness or their *eemaan* was in disarray, they would say to each other, 'Sit with us so that we may have *eemaan* for an hour'. So they would remember Allaah and remember his religious and worldly favours causing their *eemaan* to renew itself.

Again, abstaining from forbidden and indecent acts, especially, the obscenity of fornication, this is definitely a great sign for *eemaan*. The believer, because of the fear he has concerning his standing in front of his Lord, he:

وَنَهَى ٱلنَّفْسَ عَنِ ٱلْهَوَىٰ

"...restrained himself from impure evil desires and lusts."[146]

...in response to the necessity of *eemaan* and to nourish what he already possesses of *eemaan*.

In addition, observing trusts and contracts and preserving them is from the signs of *eemaan* and related in a *hadeeth*: "...*and there is no eemaan for the one who is not trustworthy.*"[*]

If you would like to know of the *eemaan* and religion of a slave, then inspect his condition: does he fulfil all of his trusts and contracts, the

---

[146] Soorah an-Naazi'aat (79):40.

[*] Related by Ahmad, 3/135; Ibn Abee Shaybah in both his *Musannaf*, 11/11 and *al-Eemaan*, pg. 5; Ibn Hibbaan in his *Saheeh*, (1/208 *al-Ihsaan*) and al-Baghawee in *Sharh as-Sunnah*, 1/75. Al-Baghawee declared, "This is a *hasan hadeeth*." It was declared *saheeh* by al-Albaanee in his *tahqeeq* of *al-Eemaan* by Ibn Abee Shaybah.

verbal and financial or trusts concerning rights? Does he observe the rights, covenants and oaths, the ones between himself and Allaah or those between himself and his fellow servants? If the answer is in the positive then he is a person of religion and *eemaan*. If however that is not the case, his religion and *eemaan* will be deficient in accordance to the level of his infringement of these obligations.

Allaah ended these *aayaat* with the issue of safeguarding the prayers with respect to their limits, rights and times. This is because preservation of this, is of similar standing to the water that flows around the garden of *eemaan*. So it irrigates it, nurtures it and produces its crop upon every occasion.

The tree of *eemaan* is in need of constant irrigation at all times; this irrigation is the maintenance of acts of obedience and worship of the day and night. It also demands the obliteration of anything that harms it, such as alien and harmful rocks and growths; this is in reference to the abstention from unlawful matters in both speech and action. Whenever these undertakings are accomplished, this garden will witness its geese and it will produce its assorted crop.

In light of this clarification, the strong effect of righteous actions on the increase of *eemaan* has become clear to us. It is also clear that the performance and increase of these acts are a tremendous cause for the increase of *eemaan*.

Shaykh al-Islaam says: "The perfection of *eemaan* is in enacting the commands of Allaah and His Messenger and refraining from the prohibitions of Allaah and His Messenger. Consequently, if one does not perform certain commandments and replaces them by embarking on certain prohibitions; this will result in a proportional decrease of *eemaan*."

Thus, prayer is *eemaan*, *hajj* is *eemaan*, *s̲adaqah* is *eemaan*, *jihaad* is *eemaan* and all the actions that Allaah has ordered His slaves with are *eemaan*. If the servant does these acts his *eemaan* will increase and the performance of these actions will be a cause for the increase of his *eemaan*, on the condition of sincerity and adherence.

Shaykh Muhammad al-'Uthaymeen, may Allaah preserve him, states: "The increase of *eemaan* has causes, some of these are: performing acts of obedience because *eemaan* increases in proportion to the fineness, type and abundance of the action. Thus the finer the action the greater will be the increase of *eemaan*; the fine aspect of the action is determined by the degree of sincerity and adherence. As for the type of action, the obligatory type is better than the recommended and some forms of worship are more emphasised and virtuous than others; the more virtuous the act of obedience is the greater will be the resultant increase in *eemaan*. As for the abundance of the action, then *eemaan* increases as a result of it because action is from *eemaan*, so it is not surprising that *eemaan* increases because of an increase of the action."[147]

In addition, other great righteous actions that increase *eemaan*, which have not yet been mentioned are *da'wah* to Allaah and keeping company with virtuous people. Because of the importance and great benefit of these two matters in the increase of *eemaan*, its discussion is imperative.

As for *da'wah* to Allaah (تعالى) and to His religion, consulting each other with the truth and patience, calling to the fundamentals of the religion, to the adherence of its laws by way of ordering the good and forbidding the evil and sincerely advising the Muslims, this is all from the incentives and causes for *eemaan*.

With this, the servant perfects himself and others, as Allaah (تعالى) has sworn by time,[148] that the whole genus of humans are in a state of loss except for the one who is categorised with four qualities: *eemaan* and righteous actions, which both constitute the perfection of the self; (thirdly,) mutual consultation with the truth, which is beneficial knowledge, righteous action and the true religion and (fourthly,) mutual consultation with patience in all of this, and with these (last) two, others are perfected.

---

[147] *Fath Rabb al-Bariyyah*, pg. 65.

[148] Refer to Soorah al-'Asr (103). [t]

This is because *da'wah* to Allaah itself and advising His servants are amongst the greatest fortifiers of *eemaan*. The person involved in *da'wah* has to work to aid this *da'wah* and establish the proofs and evidences for its realisation. He has to undertake matters from their proper channels and approach issues from their rightful paths. These issues are from the ways and channels of *eemaan*.

Shaykh al-Islaam states: "The reason for the presence of *eemaan* and its constituents sometimes traces back to the servant (himself) and at other times back to others, for example, one is destined to interact with someone who invites him to *eemaan*, orders him with good and forbids him from evil. He explains to him the signs of the religion, its proofs and evidences. He shows him what to consider, what befalls him, what to take heed from. In addition (to this), there are many other reasons."[149]

Furthermore, the reward is always from the same class as the action. So, just as the person strives to perfect his fellow servants, advises them, consults them with truth and to be patience in all this, Allaah will most definitely compensate him with rewards similar to his actions. Allaah will assist him with a light and spirit from Him and with strength of *eemaan* and *tawakkul*.

Eemaan and strong *tawakkul* on Allaah bring about victory over the enemies of the devils of men and *jinn* as Allaah (تعالى) has said:

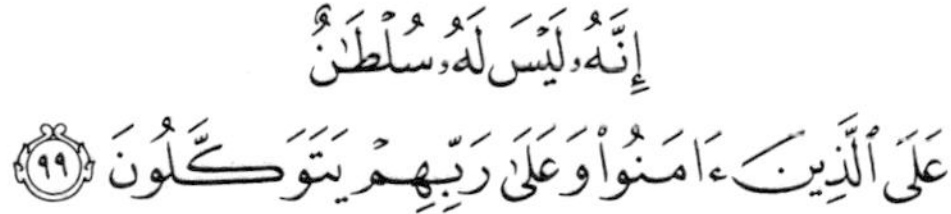

"Verily, he (i.e., *Shaytaan*) has no power over those who have *eemaan* and put their trust solely on their Lord."[150]

Moreover, this person is also occupied with aiding the truth and whoever turns to undertake something, then he will most definitely be granted certain triumphs in knowledge and *eemaan* according to his truthfulness and sincerity.

---

[149] *Al-Fataawa*, 7/650.

[150] Soorah an-Nahl (16):99.

One who commands the good and forbids the evil must therefore remain adherent to truthfulness and sincerity when commanding and forbidding in order for it to bear fruit and produce pure *eemaan* in him as well as those whom he is propagating to. He must also observe wisdom and leniency when inviting, be patient with those whom he is calling and to have knowledge of that which he is calling them to.

If these features are realised within him, his *da'wah* will bear fruit and benefit by the will of Allaah and it will be a cause for the strengthening of his *eemaan* and of those whom he is calling.

As for keeping company with virtuous people, clinging to them, accompanying them and coveting to benefit from them, this is a great cause for the increase of *eemaan*. The reason being that these type of gatherings embody reminder of Allaah, fear of Him (سبحانه) and His punishment, *targheeb*, *tarheeb* and other matters, which are of the greatest of causes towards the increase of *eemaan*.

As Allaah (تعالى) says:

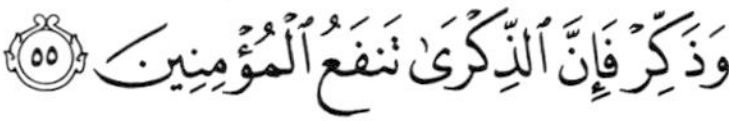

> **"And remind, for indeed, reminding benefits the believers."**[151]

Allaah (تعالى) also says:

> **"Therefore, remind, in case the reminder benefits; those who fear will remember and the wretched will avoid it."**[152]

This shows that possessors of believing hearts benefit greatly from reminders and from being in congregations of remembrance. It provokes activity and resolution within them and obligates profit and

---

[151] Soorah adh-Dhaariyaat (51):55.

[152] Soorah al-A'laa (87):9-11.

elevation. This is in stark contrast to gatherings of frivolity and foolishness, for these are immense reasons for the decrease and fading away of *eemaan*.

To this effect, our righteous predecessors were the most concerned with gatherings of remembrance and the most distant from meetings of frivolity and foolishness. Many of their statements that indicate this have preceded, like the accounts of 'Umayr Ibn Habeeb al-Khatmee and Mu'aadh Ibn Jabal, may Allaah be pleased with them.

There is another cause, with which I will end the discussion on these causes, which one must pay attention to and not neglect.

The Muslim has to train and adapt himself to fight everything that causes a decrease, weakness or disappearance of *eemaan*.

"Since, in relation to *eemaan*, just as one must enact all the causes that strengthen and develop *eemaan*, then likewise, in addition to this, one must repel the preventive matters and obstacles (towards the attainment and increase of *eemaan*). Repelling these are accomplished by the abandonment of disobedience; being repentant of the disobedience one does commit; safeguarding the limbs from the unlawful issues and opposing the trials and afflictions of misconceptions that weaken the desires of *eemaan*, which are in essence, the desire and love for good. Endeavouring after this can only be accomplished by abandoning desires that (would otherwise) negate those desires (of *eemaan*), such as desire of the soul for evil and by opposing the soul that constantly commands evil.

When the servant preserves himself from falling into the trials and tribulations of misconceptions and desires, his *eemaan* will become complete and his certainty will become strong."[153]

With Allaah, lies all *tawfeeq*.

[153] *At-Tawdeeh wa al-Bayaan* of Ibn as-Sa'dee, page 37.

Causes for the Decrease of *Eemaan*

The previous discussion centred on the causes for the increase of *eemaan*. The discussion here however, is on the causes for its decrease. Since, just as *eemaan* has causes that increase and develop *eemaan*, it also has causes that decrease and weaken it. Just as it is required of the Muslim to be aware of the causes for the increase of *eemaan* in order for him to apply them, likewise, it is demanded of him to know of the causes of its decrease so that he remains apart from them. This obligation emanates from the perspective found in the proverb:

I learnt evil, not for evil, but to guard against it

for whoever among the people is not aware of evil, will fall into it

Moreover, it has been established in the *Saheehayn* from Hudhayfah Ibn al-Yamaan, may Allaah be pleased with him, that he said: "The Companions used to ask the Messenger of Allaah (ﷺ) concerning the good and I used to ask him about the evil in fear of it afflicting me."[154]

Ibn al-Jawzee said: "Being well-versed with evil embodies an alertness against falling into it."[155]

Thus, learning the causes behind the decrease of *eemaan* and being aware of the factors that weaken it and of how to safeguard one's self from them is a vital matter, which must be looked at. In fact, gaining knowledge of these causes is no less important than learning the causes for the increase of *eemaan*.

Before I begin to mention and shed light on the causes for the decrease of *eemaan*, I would like to point out that the non-maintenance

[154] Al-Bukhaaree, 8/93 and Muslim, 3/1475.

[155] *Talbees Iblees*, page 4 and see *al-Fataawa* of Ibn Taymiyyah, 10/301 and onwards.

of the causes of the increase of *eemaan*, neglecting to strengthen it and paying no regard to this, is deemed in itself a cause from the causes that decrease *eemaan*.

To therefore disregard the aforementioned issues and not pay any attention to them, weakens and decreases the *eemaan*. So just as their preservation is a cause for increase, in like manner, their disregard is a cause for decrease.

Shaykh Muhammad al-'Uthaymeen states: "As for the decrease of *eemaan*, it has many reasons..." he then them mentioned a number of points, from them: "Abandoning obedience, for *eemaan* decreases as a result of this. This decrease will be proportional to the significance of the particular act of obedience; the more significant and emphasised it is, the greater will be the decrease resulting from not performing it. It maybe that *eemaan* vanishes in its entirety, like in the abandonment of prayer."[156]

This is shown by the saying of Allaah (تعالى):

"Indeed, he succeeds, who purifies it (i.e., his soul). And indeed, he fails, who corrupts it."[157]

This noble Qur'aanic text signifies the importance of obedience and its preservation and that it is one of the greatest reasons for the purification of the soul. In sharp contrast, it also indicates the danger of neglecting obedience and of falling into disobedience and that it is one of the greatest reasons for failure and loss.

Ibn Jareer at-Tabaree, may Allaah have mercy upon him, mentions in his *Tafseer*:

"His saying, قَدْ أَفْلَحَ مَن زَكَّىٰهَا **"Indeed, he succeeds who purifies it."** Allaah says that indeed, he succeeds who purifies his soul; so he greatly purified his soul from *kufr* and disobedience and he rectified it through righteous actions..."

[156] *Fath Rabb al-Bariyyah*, page 66.

[157] Soorah ash-Shams (91):9-10.

At-Tabaree than related some accounts from the *Salaf* that support this: He related from Qataadah, 'Whoever works good, purifies it with obedience to Allaah.' He also related from him, 'Indeed, he succeeds, who purifies his soul with righteous actions.'

He related from Ibn Zayd that he said, 'He succeeds, whom Allaah has purified his soul.'

He related from Mujaahid, Sa'eed Ibn Jubayr and 'Ikrimah, 'قَدْ أَفْلَحَ مَن زَكَّىٰهَا **"Indeed, he succeeds who purifies it."** They said: "whoever rectifies it.''[158]

Ibn al-Qayyim relates that al-Hasan al-Basree said: "He succeeds, who purifies his soul by rectifying it and directing it towards obedience of Allaah (تعالى) and he fails, who ruins it and directs it towards disobedience of Allaah (تعالى)."

He also transmits from Ibn Qutaybah that he said: "It means: he succeeds, who purifies his soul, i.e., cultivates it and elevates it by obedience, righteousness, truthfulness and doing good deeds."[159]

As for the saying of Allaah (تعالى), وَقَدْ خَابَ مَن دَسَّىٰهَا **"and indeed, he fails who corrupts it."**

Ibn Jareer states: "Allaah, may His mention be elevated, says, 'and he failed in his request, the one who corrupts it does not attain the righteousness he seeks and searches out for, i.e., Allaah corrupts it by neglecting and disparaging it, through forsaking his soul concerning guidance until he perpetrated sinful deeds and abandoned obedience to Allaah."

He then related a report from Mujaahid, that he said: "وَقَدْ خَابَ مَن دَسَّىٰهَا **'And indeed, he fails who corrupts it.'** i.e., misguided it. He relates on Sa'eed Ibn Jubayr: "i.e., he misled it.' and on Qataadah again: 'i.e., caused it to sin and debauched it.'[160]

[158] *Tafseer at-Tabaree*, 15/211-212.

[159] *Ighaathah al-Lahfaan*, 1/65.

[160] *Tafseer at-Tabaree*, 15/212-213.

Ibn al-Qayyim says: "i.e., he reduced and concealed it by abandoning actions of piety and embarking upon disobedience. The immoral one is always in a hidden place, has chronically ill conduct, is an obscure person and has a lowered head; the one who embarks upon obscene deeds has indeed corrupted his soul and suppressed it."[161]

Thus, whoever purifies his soul by performing the commandments and avoiding the prohibitions has indeed succeeded and prospered and whoever corrupts his soul by abandoning the commandments and embarking upon the prohibited has indeed lost and failed.

Regarding the causes for the decrease of *eemaan* and the factors that weaken it, they are many and of different sorts. However, in general, they are two categories and a number of factors reside under each category:

1. Internal Causes

As for the first category, it is made up of the internal causes or inherent factors, which bear effect upon the eemaan by decreasing it. These are many factors:

(i) Ignorance

This is one of the most significant causes for the decreases of *eemaan*, just as knowledge is one of the greatest causes for the increase of *eemaan*. The knowledgeable Muslim does not prefer the love and enactment of matters that harm him and cause him pain and misery to that which constitutes his benefit, success and rectification.

The ignorant person on the other hand, because of his excess ignorance and deficient knowledge, he may give preference to some of these things over that which contains his success and rectification. This is because the scales with him have been turned upside down and it is because of his feeble perception.

---

[161] *Ighaathah al-Lahfaan*, 1/65 and see *At-Tibyaan fee Aqsaam al-Qur'aan* of Ibn al-Qayyim, page 21.

Knowledge lies at the root of all good and ignorance lies at the root of all evil.

The primary reason for love of oppression, transgression, embarking upon obscene acts and committing unlawful deeds is ignorance and the corruption of knowledge, or the corruption of intent, and the corruption of intent traces back to the corruption of knowledge. Hence, ignorance and corruption of knowledge form the main and primary reason for the corruption of actions and weakness of *eemaan*.

Ibn al-Qayyim writes: "It has been purported that the corruption of intent is caused by the corruption of knowledge. Since, if the person truly knew of the harm and its implications within the detrimental action, he would not have preferred it. This is why when one has knowledge that a particular desirous and delicious food contains poison, he does not dare approach it. Thus, his knowledge of the various types of harm present within the harmful act is weak and his resolve to avoid what he could fall into as a result of committing the act is also weak.

This is why *eemaan* is in accordance to this. The one who has true *eemaan* in the Fire in the way he is supposed to have, to the extent as if he is viewing it, will not take the path that leads to it, let alone strive along that path with his might. The one who has true *eemaan* in Paradise in the way he is supposed to have, his soul will not consent to refrain from seeking it.

This is a matter that a person can see in himself concerning the benefits he strives for or the harms that he tries to deliver himself from in this world."[162]

Hence, the soul is fond of that which will harm it and not benefit it because of its ignorance of the harmful effects. In this light, one who examines the Noble Qur'aan, will find the greatest indication that ignorance is the cause for sins and obedience.

---

[162] *Ighaathah al-Lahfaan*, 3/133.

Allaah (تعالى) says:

قَالُوا۟ يَـٰمُوسَى ٱجْعَل لَّنَآ إِلَـٰهًا كَمَا لَهُمْ ءَالِهَةٌ ۚ قَالَ إِنَّكُمْ قَوْمٌ تَجْهَلُونَ ﴿١٣٨﴾

"...They said, 'O Moosa, Make for us a deity just as they have deities.' He said, 'Verily, you are a people who are ignorant."[163]

Allaah (تعالى) says:

وَلُوطًا إِذْ قَالَ لِقَوْمِهِۦٓ أَتَأْتُونَ ٱلْفَـٰحِشَةَ وَأَنتُمْ تُبْصِرُونَ ﴿٥٤﴾ أَئِنَّكُمْ لَتَأْتُونَ ٱلرِّجَالَ شَهْوَةً مِّن دُونِ ٱلنِّسَآءِ ۚ بَلْ أَنتُمْ قَوْمٌ تَجْهَلُونَ ﴿٥٥﴾

"And remember Loot. When he said to his people, 'Do you approach vile sins while you see (each other). Do you approach men in your lusts rather than women. Rather, you are a people who are ignorant.'"[164]

Allaah (تعالى) says:

قُلْ أَفَغَيْرَ ٱللَّهِ تَأْمُرُوٓنِّىٓ أَعْبُدُ أَيُّهَا ٱلْجَـٰهِلُونَ ﴿٦٤﴾

"Say, 'Do you order me to worship other than Allaah, O you ignorant people.'"[165]

Allaah (تعالى) says:

وَقَرْنَ فِى بُيُوتِكُنَّ وَلَا تَبَرَّجْنَ تَبَرُّجَ ٱلْجَـٰهِلِيَّةِ ٱلْأُولَىٰ

"And stay in your houses and do not display yourselves like that of the times of ignorance..."[166]

Additionally, there are other texts of this like, which show that the greatest reason for the *shirk*, *kufr*, iniquities and embarking on sins that

---

163 Soorah al-A'raaf (7):138.

164 Soorah an-Naml (27):54-55.

165 Soorah az-Zumar (39):64.

166 Soorah al-Ahzaab (33):33.

people fall into, is ignorance of Allaah, His names, His attributes and of His reward and punishment.

For this reason, whoever disobeys Allaah and commits some form of sin is an ignorant person, as understood from the *Salaf* in the explanation of His (تعالى) saying:

إِنَّمَا ٱلتَّوْبَةُ عَلَى ٱللَّهِ لِلَّذِينَ يَعْمَلُونَ ٱلسُّوٓءَ بِجَهَٰلَةٍ
ثُمَّ يَتُوبُونَ مِن قَرِيبٍ فَأُو۟لَٰٓئِكَ يَتُوبُ ٱللَّهُ عَلَيْهِمْ ۗ وَكَانَ
ٱللَّهُ عَلِيمًا حَكِيمًا ﴿١٧﴾

"Allaah only accepts the repentance of those who do evil out of ignorance and repent soon afterwards. It is they to whom Allaah will forgive and Allaah is ever All-Knowing, All-Wise."[167]

And in His (تعالى) saying:

كَتَبَ رَبُّكُمْ عَلَىٰ نَفْسِهِ ٱلرَّحْمَةَ ۖ أَنَّهُۥ مَنْ عَمِلَ مِنكُمْ سُوٓءًۢا
بِجَهَٰلَةٍ ثُمَّ تَابَ مِنۢ بَعْدِهِۦ وَأَصْلَحَ فَأَنَّهُۥ غَفُورٌ رَّحِيمٌ ﴿٥٤﴾

"...Your Lord has written Mercy for Himself, so that, if any of you does evil out of ignorance, and thereafter repents and does righteous good deeds, then surely, He is oft-Forgiving, Most Merciful."[168]

And His saying:

ثُمَّ إِنَّ رَبَّكَ لِلَّذِينَ عَمِلُوا۟ ٱلسُّوٓءَ بِجَهَٰلَةٍ ثُمَّ تَابُوا۟ مِنۢ
بَعْدِ ذَٰلِكَ وَأَصْلَحُوٓا۟ إِنَّ رَبَّكَ مِنۢ بَعْدِهَا لَغَفُورٌ رَّحِيمٌ ﴿١١٩﴾

"Moreover, your Lord is towards those who do evil out of ignorance and afterward repent and do righteous deeds, verily, your Lord thereafter, is Oft-Forgiving, Most Merciful."[169]

---

[167] Soorah an-Nisaa' (4):17.

[168] Soorah al-An'aam (6):54.

[169] Soorah an-Nahl (16):119.

The meaning of **"...out of ignorance..."** in these *aayaat*, i.e., out of the doer's ignorance of its consequences and obligation of the anger and punishment of Allaah. It is his ignorance of the fact that Allaah sees and observes him and ignorance of the decrease of *eemaan* that returns to him or its complete disappearance.

Thus, everyone who disobeys Allaah, then he is ignorant in this respect, even if he is aware of the prohibition. Indeed, having knowledge of the prohibition is a condition for it to be regarded as disobedience and punishable.[170]

A group of the *Salaf* reported this type of understanding on the aayah. At-Tabaree related several of these reports in his *tafseer*. He relates on Aboo al-'Aaliyah that he used to mention that the Companions used to say: "Every sin that a slave is afflicted with; it is out of ignorance."

Qataadah relates: "The Companions assembled and concluded that concerning everything that Allaah is disobeyed with, it is out of ignorance, whether intentionally or not."

Mujaahid said: "Everyone who disobeys his Lord; he is an ignorant person, until he comes away from his disobedience."

He also said: "Anyone who commits disobedience of Allaah, that is ignorance on his behalf until he leaves off his disobedience."

As-Siddee states: "As long as he is disobeying Allaah, then he is an ignorant person."

Ibn Zayd says: "Every person who commits some form of disobedience of Allaah, then he will always be an ignorant person until he retracts from it."[171]

Hence, ignorance is a dangerous disease and a lethal illness. It draws on the person numerous disastrous calamities and consequences.

---

[170] *Tafseer Ibn as-Sa'dee*, 2/39.

[171] Refer to these reports and others in *Tafseer at-Tabaree*, 3/229 and 5/209; *Tafseer al-Baghawee*, 1/407; *al-Fataawa* of Ibn Taymiyyah, 7/22 and *Tafseer Ibn Katheer*, 1/463.

If this disease takes command of him and dominates a person, do not even bother to question his devastation. For he will be sinking into the darkness of disobedience and sins, deviating from Allaah's straight path and giving way to the demands of misconceptions and desires. Unless the mercy of Allaah embraces and emends him with the aid of the heart, the light of vision and key to all good: beneficial knowledge, which produces righteous action. As there is no other cure for this illness besides knowledge.

This disease will not separate from the person except if Allaah teaches him that which will benefit him and inspires him with good conduct.

Therefore, whomever Allaah desires good, He will teach him that which will benefit him, grant him understanding of the religion and enlighten him about what constitutes his success and happiness, so Allaah will lead him away from ignorance. Whenever Allaah does not desire good for a person, He leaves him upon his ignorance.

We ask Allaah to aid our hearts with knowledge and *eemaan* and that He protects us from ignorance and transgression.

ii. Heedlessness, Aversion and Forgetfulness

These three matters constitute immense cause for the decrease of *eemaan*. One who is stricken with heedlessness, troubled with forgetfulness and turns away, his *eemaan* will decrease in accordance to the presence of some or all of these three matters. It will impose on him ailment of the heart or its death because of its prevalence by misconceptions and desires.

Concerning heedlessness, Allaah has condemned it in His Book and He mentioned that it is a reprehensible mannerism, which is from the code and conduct of the disbelievers and hypocrites. Allaah also warns against it very severely. Allaah (تعالى) says:

وَلَقَدْ ذَرَأْنَا لِجَهَنَّمَ كَثِيرًا مِّنَ ٱلْجِنِّ وَٱلْإِنسِ ۖ لَهُمْ قُلُوبٌ
لَّا يَفْقَهُونَ بِهَا وَلَهُمْ أَعْيُنٌ لَّا يُبْصِرُونَ بِهَا وَلَهُمْ ءَاذَانٌ لَّا يَسْمَعُونَ
بِهَآ ۚ أُو۟لَٰٓئِكَ كَٱلْأَنْعَٰمِ بَلْ هُمْ أَضَلُّ ۚ أُو۟لَٰٓئِكَ هُمُ ٱلْغَٰفِلُونَ ﴿١٧٩﴾

"And surely, We have created for Hell, many (a people) from the *jinn* and mankind. They have hearts with which they understand not, they have eyes with which they see not and they have ears with which they hear not: they are like cattle. Rather, they are even more astray. They indeed, are the heedless ones."[172]

Allaah (تعالى) says:

إِنَّ ٱلَّذِينَ لَا يَرْجُونَ لِقَآءَنَا وَرَضُوا۟ بِٱلْحَيَوٰةِ ٱلدُّنْيَا وَٱطْمَأَنُّوا۟
بِهَا وَٱلَّذِينَ هُمْ عَنْ ءَايَـٰتِنَا غَـٰفِلُونَ ﴿٧﴾ أُو۟لَـٰٓئِكَ مَأْوَىٰهُمُ
ٱلنَّارُ بِمَا كَانُوا۟ يَكْسِبُونَ ﴿٨﴾

"Verily, those who hope not for their meeting with Us, but are pleased and satisfied with the life of the present world and those who are heedless of our signs; those, their abode will be the Fire because of what they used to earn."[173]

Allaah (تعالى) says:

وَإِنَّ كَثِيرًا مِّنَ ٱلنَّاسِ عَنْ ءَايَـٰتِنَا لَغَـٰفِلُونَ ﴿٩٢﴾

"...and verily, many among mankind are heedless of our signs."[174]

Allaah (تعالى) also says:

يَعْلَمُونَ ظَـٰهِرًا مِّنَ ٱلْحَيَوٰةِ ٱلدُّنْيَا وَهُمْ عَنِ ٱلْـَٔاخِرَةِ هُمْ غَـٰفِلُونَ

"They know only the outside appearance of the life of this world whilst they are heedless of the Hereafter."[175]

[172] Soorah al-A'raaf (7):179.

[173] Soorah Yoonus (10):7-8.

[174] Soorah Yoonus (10):92.

[175] Soorah ar-Room (30):7.

Allaah (تعالى) also says to His Messenger(ﷺ):

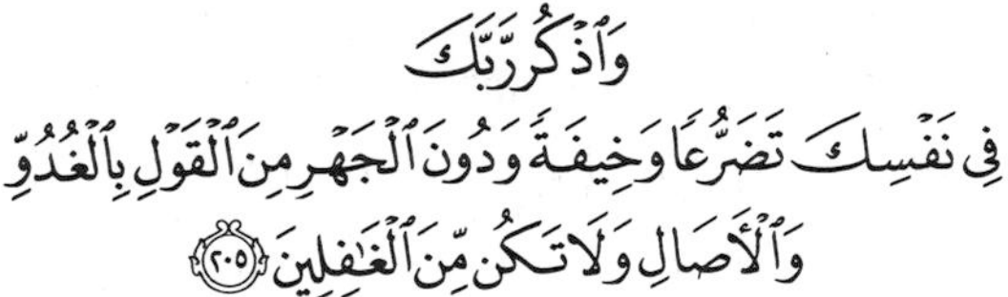

"And remember your Lord (by your tongue and) within yourself, humbly and with fear without loudness in words in the mornings and in the afternoons and be not of those who are heedless."[176]

Thus heedlessness, which is defined as negligence that occurs as a result of a lack of care and alertness, is a dangerous disease. If it afflicts a person and overwhelms him, he will not bother with obedience of Allaah, His remembrance and worship. Instead, he will be occupied with matters of distraction, which distance him from the remembrance of Allaah. Moreover, if he does perform certain deeds in obedience to Allaah, he does them in an inadequate state and inappropriate manner, so his actions are void of humility, humbleness, repentance, fear, tranquillity, truthfulness and sincerity.

Thus, these are some of the bad effects that heedlessness has on *eemaan*.

As for aversion, Allaah mentions in the noble Qur'aan that it has many ill effects and destructive results and consequences. Of these, Allaah has described the one who turns away as being the most oppressive and that he is amongst the criminals, as Allaah (تعالى) says:

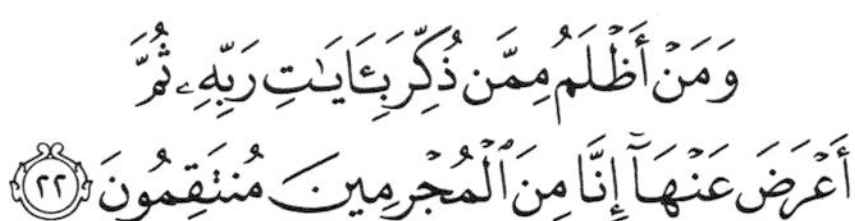

"And who is more oppressive than one who is reminded of the signs of His Lord, then he turns away from them? Verily, We shall extract retribution from the criminals."[177]

---

[176] Soorah al-A'raaf (7):205.

[177] Soorah as-Sajdah (32):22.

Allaah also informs that He has set a veil and locks upon the heart of the one who turns away, so he does not comprehend or come upon the right path, ever, as in Allaah's statement:

وَمَنْ أَظْلَمُ مِمَّن ذُكِّرَ بِـَٔايَٰتِ رَبِّهِۦ فَأَعْرَضَ عَنْهَا وَنَسِىَ مَا قَدَّمَتْ يَدَاهُ ۚ إِنَّا جَعَلْنَا عَلَىٰ قُلُوبِهِمْ أَكِنَّةً أَن يَفْقَهُوهُ وَفِىٓ ءَاذَانِهِمْ وَقْرًا ۖ وَإِن تَدْعُهُمْ إِلَى ٱلْهُدَىٰ فَلَن يَهْتَدُوٓا۟ إِذًا أَبَدًا ﴿٥٧﴾

"And who is more oppressive than one who is reminded of the signs of His Lord, but turns away from them forgetting what (deeds) his hands have sent forth. Truly, We have set veils over their hearts lest they should understand it (i.e., the Qur'aan), and in their ears, deafness. And if you call them to guidance, even then they will never be guided."[178]

This aversion on the person's part also causes a life of hardship and constriction in this world and the Hereafter. Allaah says:

وَمَنْ أَعْرَضَ عَن ذِكْرِى فَإِنَّ لَهُۥ مَعِيشَةً ضَنكًا وَنَحْشُرُهُۥ يَوْمَ ٱلْقِيَٰمَةِ أَعْمَىٰ ﴿١٢٤﴾

"But whoever turns away from My reminder, verily, for him is a life of hardship, and We shall raise him up blind on the Day of Resurrection."[179]

Allaah (سبحانه) also informs that the one who turns away from the remembrance of Allaah is assigned associates from amongst the *Shayaa<u>t</u>een*, whom thereafter corrupt his religion, as Allaah says:

وَمَن يَعْشُ عَن ذِكْرِ ٱلرَّحْمَٰنِ نُقَيِّضْ لَهُۥ شَيْطَٰنًا فَهُوَ لَهُۥ قَرِينٌ

"And whosoever turns away from the remembrance of the Most Beneficent, We shall appoint for him a *Shayt̲aan* to be an (intimate) companion."[180]

---

[178] Soorah al-Kahf (18):57.

[179] Soorah T̲aa Haa (20):124.

[180] Soorah az-Zukhruf (43):36.

Furthermore, Allaah informs that the one who turns away will bear a heavy burden of sins on the Day of Resurrection and that he will enter a severe punishment.

Allaah says:

مَّنْ أَعْرَضَ عَنْهُ فَإِنَّهُۥ يَحْمِلُ يَوْمَ ٱلْقِيَـٰمَةِ وِزْرًا

> **"Whoever turns away from it (i.e., the Qur'aan), verily, he will bear a heavy burden (of sins) on the Day of Resurrection."**[181]

Allaah also says:

وَمَن يُعْرِضْ عَن ذِكْرِ رَبِّهِۦ يَسْلُكْهُ عَذَابًا صَعَدًا ﴿١٧﴾

> **"...and whosoever turns away from the reminder of his Lord, He will cause him to enter into a severe torment."**[182]

Similarly, there are many other *aayaat* in which Allaah (ﷻ) talks of the dangers and harms of aversion. The most dangerous of these is the fact that it poses as an obstacle and barrier to acquiring *eemaan* for the one who does not yet believe and that it weakens the *eemaan* of one who already believes.

It is the extent of the person's aversion that will determine his allotment of these consequences and dangers.

As for forgetfulness, which is defined as one leaving the exactness of that which he has already safeguarded. This occurs because of the weakness of his heart, or as a result of negligence on his behalf or out of deliberate intention until any trace of it is removed from his heart.[183]

This has a profound effect upon *eemaan*. It is a cause for its weakness; its presence decreases acts of obedience and greatens acts of disobedience.

The forgetfulness mentioned in the Qur'aan is of two types. The first type is one that a person is not excused for. This is in reference to the type that occurs deliberately, as in His saying:

---

[181] Soorah Taa-Haa (20):100.

[182] Soorah al-Jinn (72):17.

[183] *Basaa'ir Dhaway at-Tamyeez* of al-Fayroozabaadee, 5/49.

وَلَا تَكُونُوا۟ كَٱلَّذِينَ نَسُوا۟ ٱللَّهَ فَأَنسَىٰهُمْ أَنفُسَهُمْ

> **"And do not be like those who forget Allaah, thereupon Allaah caused them to forget their own selves."**[184]

The second type is one in which the person is excused. This is in reference to when the reason for the forgetfulness does not emanate from the person (whereby he intends that), as in the saying of Allaah (تعالى):

رَبَّنَا لَا تُؤَاخِذْنَآ إِن نَّسِينَآ أَوْ أَخْطَأْنَا

> **"...Our Lord, do not hold us to account if we forget or commit mistakes..."**[185]

It has been recorded in a hadeeth (in connection to this aayah) that Allaah (تعالى) said: "I have done so."[186][187]

The Muslim is required to fight his soul and to distance it from falling into this, so that he does not become harmed in his religion and *eemaan*.

iii. Committing Disobedience and Embarking upon Sinful Deeds

The harm and bad effect of this factor upon *eemaan* is well known to all. Thus *eemaan*, as stated by more than one of the *Salaf*, 'increases with obedience and decreases with disobedience'. Just as accomplishing the obligatory and recommended deeds that Allaah has ordained increases *eemaan*, then likewise, performing the forbidden and disliked deeds that Allaah has not enjoined decreases *eemaan*.

---

[184] Soorah al-Hashr (59):19.

[185] Soorah al-Baqarah (2):286.

[186] i.e., Allaah will not hold to us to account if we forget or commit mistakes... - and all praise is for Allaah. [t]

[187] Related by Muslim, 1/116 from the *hadeeth* of Ibn 'Abbaas, may Allaah be pleased with him.

However, sins vary greatly with respect to their rank, the evils they entail and the intensity of their harm. This is as Ibn al-Qayyim has mentioned: "Without doubt, kufr, *fusooq* and disobedience are of levels just as *eemaan* and righteous actions are of levels. Allaah (تعالى) says:

هُمْ دَرَجَٰتٌ عِندَ ٱللَّهِ ۗ وَٱللَّهُ بَصِيرٌۢ بِمَا يَعْمَلُونَ ﴿١٦٣﴾

"They are in varying grades before Allaah and Allaah is All-Seer of what they do."[188]

He says:

وَلِكُلٍّ دَرَجَٰتٌ مِّمَّا عَمِلُوا۟ ۚ وَمَا رَبُّكَ بِغَٰفِلٍ عَمَّا يَعْمَلُونَ ﴿١٣٢﴾

"For all there will be degrees, according to that which they did. And your Lord is not unaware of what they do."[189]

He says:

إِنَّمَا ٱلنَّسِىٓءُ زِيَادَةٌ فِى ٱلْكُفْرِ

"The postponing (of a sacred month) is indeed an addition to *kufr*..."[190]

He also says:

فَأَمَّا ٱلَّذِينَ ءَامَنُوا۟ فَزَادَتْهُمْ إِيمَٰنًا وَهُمْ يَسْتَبْشِرُونَ ﴿١٢٤﴾ وَأَمَّا ٱلَّذِينَ فِى قُلُوبِهِم مَّرَضٌ فَزَادَتْهُمْ رِجْسًا إِلَىٰ رِجْسِهِمْ

"...As for those who believe, it has increased their *eemaan* and they rejoice. But as for those whose hearts is a disease, it will add *rijs*[191] to their *rijs*..."[192]

[188] Soorah Aal-'Imraan (3):163.

[189] Soorah al-An'aam (6):132.

[190] Soorah at-Tawbah (9):37

[191] i.e., suspicion, doubt and disbelief. [t]

[192] Soorah at-Tawbah (9):124-125.

Statements of this kind are many in the Qur'aan."[193]

The Qur'aan and *Sunnah* show that sins are of major and minor types. Allaah (تعالى) says:

إِن تَجْتَنِبُوا۟ كَبَآئِرَ مَا تُنْهَوْنَ عَنْهُ نُكَفِّرْ
عَنكُمْ سَيِّـَٔاتِكُمْ وَنُدْخِلْكُم مُّدْخَلًا كَرِيمًا ﴿٣١﴾

> **"And if you avoid the major of the sins that you are forbidden from, We shall remit for you your (minor) sins and admit you to a noble entrance."**[194]

Allaah (تعالى) also says:

ٱلَّذِينَ يَجْتَنِبُونَ كَبَـٰٓئِرَ ٱلْإِثْمِ وَٱلْفَوَٰحِشَ إِلَّا ٱللَّمَمَ

> **"Those who avoid major sins and *al-Fawaahish* except the small faults..."**[195]

It is recorded in *Saheeh Muslim*, that Aboo Hurayrah, may Allaah be pleased with him, relates the Messenger of Allaah (ﷺ) as saying: *"The five prayers, the Friday prayer to the (next) Friday prayer and Ramadaan to (the next) Ramadaan; they expiate all (sins committed) between them as long as the major ones are avoided."*[196]

As recorded in the *Saheehayn*, 'Abdur-Rahmaan Ibn Abee Bakrah relates from his father that he said: "We were with the Messenger of Allaah (ﷺ) when he questioned three times, *'Shall I not inform you of the greatest of the major sins? Committing shirk with Allaah, disobedience to parents and issuing a false testimony.'*"[197]

Also recorded in the *Saheehayn*, the Messenger of Allaah (ﷺ) was asked, 'Which sin is the greatest before Allaah?' He replied, *'That you ascribe to Allaah an equal whilst it is He who created you.'* It was asked,

---

[193] *Ighaathah al-Lahfaan*, 2/142.

[194] Soorah an-Nisaa' (4):31.

[195] Soorah an-Najm (53):32.

[196] *Saheeh Muslim*, 1/209.

[197] Al-Bukhaaree, (10/405 *Fath*) and Muslim, 1/91.

'Then which?' He said, *'That you kill your child in fear that he will also need nourishment alongside you.'* It was asked, 'Then which?' He answered, *'That you have a sexual relationship with the wife of your neighbour.'*[198]

Many other texts also show the varying levels of sins and that they are classified into major and minor ones.

Furthermore, from another perspective, these sins can be classified into four categories: ***Malikiyyah***, ***Shaytaaniyyah***, ***Sab'iyyah*** and ***Baheemiyyah***; all sins can be classified under these types.

Malikiyyah sins are committed when one takes upon himself qualities of Lordship, which are not befitting for him, such as majesty, pride, domination, subjugation, highness, enslavement of people and other qualities of this type. Sins belonging to this category are of the most serious type.

As for *Shaytaaniyyah* sins, it is by resembling *Shaytaan* in envy, oppression, cheating, hatred, deception, plotting evil, ordering disobedience of Allaah and beautifying it, prohibiting obedience of Allaah and censuring it, committing innovations in the religion of Allaah and the call to innovations and deviation. This category is placed second to the first type with respect to its harms, even though its harms are lesser.

Sab'iyyah sins are sins of transgression, anger, spilling blood, pouncing upon the weak and incapable. This gives birth to many types of harms to fellow humans and boldness towards committing oppression and transgression.

As for *Baheemiyyah* sins, examples of this are gluttony and the desire to satisfy lusts of the stomach and genital organs. This gives rise to fornication, adultery, theft, consumption of wealth belonging to orphans, miserliness, avarice, cowardice, restlessness, impatience and much more besides these.

---

[198] Al-Bukhaaree, (12/187 *Fath*) and Muslim, 1/91, from the *hadeeth* of Ibn Mas'ood, may Allaah be pleased with him.

This particular category is where most of the sins are perpetrated by people because of their incapability of committing sins of the *Saba'iyyah* and *Malikiyyah* type. It is from this category where they enter into the remaining categories, since this leads them to the rest by the reigns. Thus, as a result of this category, they enter into the area of *Saba'iyyah* sins, then the *Shaytaaniyyah*, then finally, towards contesting the Lordship and committing *shirk* in the oneness of Allaah.

In any case, these matters show us that sins vary in their effect upon *eemaan* and upon its decrement and weakening of it.

This diversity of sins and of their effect upon *eemaan* trace back to a variety of considerations. Some of these are: the class of the sin, its amount, the degree of its harmful effects, the place, the time, with regard to its doer and other such considerations.

Ibn al-Qayyim, may Allaah have mercy upon him, says: "On the whole, the levels of *al-Faahishah* (i.e., lewd and illicit deeds) are determined by their corresponding evils. Thus, the issue of a man who befriends a woman or a woman who befriends a man is deemed less evil than the issue of a man or woman who has an (illegal) sexual relationship.

The one who does the crime in secret is less sinful than the one who does it publicly. The one who conceals his sin is less sinful than the one who relates it publicly to the people; this one is far removed from receiving well being and pardon from Allaah...

Likewise, having a sexual encounter with a woman who has no husband is less sinful than having a sexual encounter with one who has a husband, because of the oppression and transgression it entails against the husband as well as ruining his bed. The sin of this person can be greater or lesser than the mere sin of fornication.

To have a sexual encounter with the wife of a neighbour is more severe than having a sexual encounter with one who is far from home, because of its connection to harming the neighbour and not maintaining the instruction of Allaah and His Messenger with regard to the neighbour.

Similarly, having a sexual relationship with the wife of a soldier on Allaah's cause is worse than having a sexual relationship with the wife of another...

Just as its levels differ in relation to the person one has a sexual encounter with, then likewise, it also differs according to the place, the time, the circumstances and the doer.

To fornicate or commit adultery for example, in the days and nights of Ramadaan is more sinful than at any other time. Its occurrence in the blessed and virtuous places is more sinful than in any other places.

As for its difference in relation to its doer, it being committed by a free person is more vile than it being committed by a slave. This is why the punishment of the slave is half of that of the free person. It is more repugnant from the married person than the virgin; likewise the same applies for the old person in relation to the young person.

It is more repulsive from the scholar than from the ignorant, because of the former's awareness of its abhorrence and consequences and of having embarked upon it with insight, and it is worse from one who is able to do without it than from one who is poor and weak.

However, presence of particular matters, which when associated to the types of sins that are less sinful, can deem them even greater sins than those that were initially more sinful.

For example, if one associates to this *faahishah*, a type of passionate love, which imposes the heart to be occupied with the loved one; deifying this person; glorifying, being humble and subservient to the beloved and placing forward obedience of the beloved and that which he or she orders over and above obedience to Allaah (تعالى) and His Messenger.

Hence, the matters that become connected to the love and glorification of this intimate companion, to the allegiance of whom the companion shows allegiance to, to the enmity towards whom the companion shows enmity towards and towards loving and hating that which the companion loves and hates are such that they can have a more harmful effect upon the person than simply embarking upon the lewd sin

Shaykh Muhammad al-'Uthaymeen states: "As for the decrease of *eemaan*, it has causes:

1. Committing acts of disobedience. *Eemaan* decreases according to the class of sin, its amount, the indifference the person has towards it and the strength or weakness of the incentive to perpetrate it.

As for its class and amount; the decrease of *eemaan* by major sins is greater than that by the minor sins. The decrement of *eemaan* by killing a soul unlawfully is greater than (illegally) devouring valued wealth. Its decrease by two acts of disobedience is greater than one act of disobedience and so on.

As for being indifferent to the sin; if an act of disobedience emanates from a heart that thinks little of who it is disobeying and has little fear of Him, then the resultant decrease will be greater than if it were to emanate from a heart that glorifies Allaah (تعالى) and is very fearful of Him except that an act of disobedience inadvertently occurs from him.

Concerning the strength of the motive for committing the sin; if an act of disobedience emerges from a person whose incentives for doing the sin are weak, then the resultant decrease of his *eemaan* will be much greater than if it were to emerge from one whose incentives for doing the sin are strong.

This is why the display of arrogance by a poor person and an illegal sexual encounter by an old person are more sinful than the display of arrogance by a rich person and an illegal sexual encounter by a young person. As in the *hadeeth*:[199] *"Three (types of people) whom Allaah will not speak to. He will not look at them on the Day of Resurrection or sanctify them and they will have a painful punishment."*

[199] Related by at-Tabaraanee in *al-Kabeer*, 2/301; al-Bayhaqee in *ash-Shu'ab*, 3/220. Al-Haythamee declares in *Majma' az-Zawaa'id*, 4/78: "Its narrators are narrators of *as-Saheeh*." Al-Albaanee declared it *saheeh*, see *Saheeh al-Jaami'*, 3/74.

Mentioned amongst these three are the grey-haired fornicator and the poor person who is arrogant, because of the lack of strong motives they have for embarking on these disobedient acts."[200]

With what has preceded, the conclusion is that sins decrease *eemaan* and that the amount of decrease varies in accordance to a multitude of considerations. Some of these are:

1. The class of the sin
2. The degree of its harmful effects
3. The amount
4. The place and time
5. The indifference towards it
6. The doer

The explanation of this has already preceded, and with Allaah lies all *tawfeeq*.

Some matters that protect a person from sins and help him to remain distant from them and to not fall into them are the knowledge of their dangers, what they give rise to, their evil consequences and extreme harms.

Ibn al-Qayyim mentions in this respect a brief and yet more than adequate statement, which is to the point. He says: "Lack of *tawfeeq*; incorrectness of opinion; concealment of truth (from him); corruption of the heart, lack of remembrance, squandering of time; dislike of creation (of him); alienation between the servant and his Lord; prevention of supplications being answered; hardness of heart; the exclusion of blessings in one's sustenance and life; deprivation of knowledge; the apparel of degradation; humiliation subjected by the enemy; constriction of the chest; being put to trial with evil companionship who corrupt the heart and waste time; lengthy anxiety and sorrow; hardship of life and gloominess of circumstance... are a result of

[200] *Fath al-Bariyyah*, page 65.

disobedience and negligence of the remembrance of Allaah, which is comparable (in magnitude) to the vegetation that is produced by water and the burning that is caused by fire. The opposites of these matters arise from actions of obedience.'"[201]

iv. The Soul that Greatly Commands Evil

This is a condemned soul, which Allaah placed inside the individual. It orders him with every evil, invites him to all perils and guides him to every vulgarity.

This is its nature and that is its trait, except for the soul that Allaah grants *tawfeeq* and which He makes firm and assists. None has been saved from the evil of his soul except by the *tawfeeq* of Allaah, as Allaah (تعالى) says relating from the wife of al-'Azeez:

وَمَآ أُبَرِّئُ نَفْسِيٓۚ إِنَّ ٱلنَّفْسَ لَأَمَّارَةُۢ بِٱلسُّوٓءِ إِلَّا مَا رَحِمَ
رَبِّيٓۚ إِنَّ رَبِّي غَفُورٞ رَّحِيمٞ ٥٣

> **"And I free not myself (from the blame). Verily, the soul does indeed incline greatly to evil, except when my Lord bestows His Mercy (upon whom He wills). Verily, my Lord is Oft-Forgiving, Most Merciful."**[202]

Allaah (تعالى) says:

وَلَوْلَا فَضْلُ ٱللَّهِ عَلَيْكُمْ وَرَحْمَتُهُۥ مَا زَكَىٰ مِنكُم مِّنْ أَحَدٍ أَبَدًا

> **"...And had it not been for the Grace of Allaah and His Mercy on you, not one of you would ever have been pure..."**[203]

Allaah (تعالى) also says to the most honourable and beloved creation to Him:

---

[201] *Al-Fawaa'id*, page 62. Also see *al-Jawaab al-Kaafee* of Ibn al-Qayyim, page 46 and onwards.

[202] Soorah Yoosuf (12):53.

[203] Soorah an-Noor (24):21.

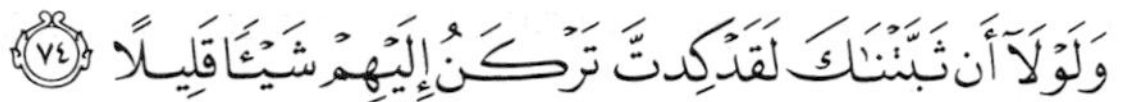

"And had We not made you stand firm, you would nearly have inclined to them a little."[204]

Furthermore, the Prophet (ﷺ) used to teach them (i.e., the people) the 'Speech of Need' (*Khutbah al-Haajah*): *"All praise is for Allaah; we praise Him, seek His aid and forgiveness. We seek refuge with Allaah from the* ***evil of our souls*** *and from the wickedness of our actions. Whosoever Allaah guides, then none can misguide him and whosoever Allaah misguides, then none can guide him…"*[205]

Thus, evil is concealed within the soul and it necessitates actions of evil. If Allaah lets the servant have his own way with his soul, he will perish at the evil of his soul and the evil actions that it sanctions. If Allaah on the other hand, grants the servant *tawfeeq* and assists him, he will deliver him from all of this.

Allaah has made in contrast to this soul, a soul that is content.[206] If the soul that constantly commands evil urges the servant with something, the content soul prohibits him from it. The person at times obeys this

---

[204] Soorah al-Israa (17):74.

[205] This speech has been related by Aboo Daawood, 2/237, an-Nasaa'iee, 3/105 and others. Refer to al-Albaanee's treatise, *'Khutbah al-Haajah'* for he gathered all the narrations and wordings of this speech.

[206] i.e., not another soul but a different characteristic of the same soul. Al-Qaadee Ibn Abee al-'Izz al-Hanafee, may Allaah have mercy upon him says in his commentary to al-Imaam at-Tahaawee's treatise on *'aqeedah*: *"Many people have recorded that the son of Aadam has three souls: a content soul (mutma'innah), a soul that reproaches much (lawwaamah) and a soul that greatly orders evil (ammaarah), and that some people are characterised by a particular one and others by another one. As Allaah (تعالى) has said:*

يَٰٓأَيَّتُهَا ٱلنَّفْسُ ٱلْمُطْمَئِنَّةُ ﴿٢٧﴾ **"O (you) soul that is content (*mutma'innah*)…"** [al-Fajr (89):28]

وَلَآ أُقْسِمُ بِٱلنَّفْسِ ٱللَّوَّامَةِ ﴿٢﴾ **"And I swear by the self-reproaching (*lawwaamah*) soul."** [al-Qiyaamah (75):2]

إِنَّ ٱلنَّفْسَ لَأَمَّارَةٌۢ بِٱلسُّوٓءِ **"…Verily, the soul does indeed incline greatly to evil…"** [Yoosuf (12):53]

The precise determination however is that it is one soul, which has (different) characteristics. Thus, it greatly encourages evil. If it becomes opposed by eemaan it becomes =

soul, and at other times obeys the other; he himself is one of the two that is prevalent over him.

Ibn al-Qayyim, may Allaah have mercy upon him, states: "Allaah (سبحانه) has assembled two souls: a soul that greatly orders (evil) and a soul that is content, and they are hostile towards one another. Whenever one diminishes, the other strengthens. Whenever one takes pleasure in something the other suffers pain as a result of it. Nothing is more difficult for the soul that constantly encourages evil than performing deeds for Allaah and preferring His pleasure to its own desire and there is nothing more beneficial to it than Allaah. Likewise, there is nothing more difficult upon the content soul than performing deeds for other than Allaah and that which the incentives of desire bring about, and there is nothing more harmful to it than desire... and the war is continuous, it cannot come to an end until it completes its appointed time from this world."[207]

Hence, there is nothing more harmful to a person's *eemaan* and religion than his soul that constantly commands evil, whose standing and description is such. It is a primary reason and effective and active constituent that weakens *eemaan*, unsettles it and impairs it.

As such, it becomes imperative for the one who seeks to safeguard his *eemaan* from diminution and weakness to tend to the matter of calling his soul to account, admonishing it and to increase in censuring it, so that he can deliver himself from its adverse and devastating consequences and ends.

Calling one's self to account is of two types: a type (that occurs) before the action and a type (that occurs) after the action.

= one that reproaches often; it commits a sin then censures its doer and reproaches with regard to doing or not doing an action. If the eemaan strengthens, it then becomes one that is content..."

Refer to *Sharh al-'Aqeedah at-Tahaawiyyah* by Ibn Abee al-'Izz al-Hanafee, pg. 569. Checked by Dr. 'Abdullaah Ibn 'Abdul-Muhsin At-Turki and Shu'ayb al-Arna'oot, 2nd print 1413H, *Mu'sassah Ar-Risaalah*, Beirut. [t]

[207] *Al-Jawaab al-Kaafee* of Ibn al-Qayyim, pg. 184-185.

As for the first type, it is to take a stance when one first has an intention and desire, and not to embark upon the action until it becomes clear to him that performing that action outweighs leaving it.

As for the second type, which is to take account of one's soul after the action, this is of three sorts:

The first is to call it to account over any obedience in which it has fallen short with regard to the right of Allaah (تعالى), whereby it has not performed it in the manner required.

The second is to call his soul to account over every action, which had he not undertaken would actually have better than having embarked upon it.

The third is that he calls his soul to account for every permissible and habitual action; why did he embark upon it? Was his intention behind the action for Allaah and the home of the Hereafter, so that he be profitable? Or did he desire the world and its immediate and instant (pleasures)? If so he would lose out on that profit and that achievement will pass him by.

The greatest harm upon the servant is negligence, to forgo calling oneself to take account, to let oneself go, to take things lightly and accommodate them. This will eventually lead him to destruction and this is the state of the people of delusion: one of them shuts their eyes to consequences, lets matters take their course and depends upon attaining pardon (from Allaah). Thus, he neglects calling himself to account and pondering over the outcomes. When he does behave in this manner, committing sins become an effortless matter for him, he feels at ease with it and it becomes difficult for him to break away from his habitual sinning.

The sum and substance of this is for the person to first call himself to account over the obligatory duties. If he finds deficiency in this regard, he amends this either by repayment or rectification. He then calls himself to account over prohibited matters. If he knows that he has perpetrated something prohibited, he amends this through repentance, seeking forgiveness and enacting good deeds that wipe such bad deeds away. He then calls himself to account over heedlessness. If it is the case that he has been careless of that which he was created for, he amends this through remembrance and turning to Allaah. He then calls himself to account over what he has spoken, or where his feet have taken him, or what his hands have struck out at or what his ears have listened out to: What did you intend from this? Who did you do it for?

He must know that for every movement and utterance he makes, two registers have to be set up: a register titled 'Who did you do it for?' and (the second register titled) 'In what manner did you do it?'

The first (register) is a question on sincerity and the second is a question on conformity (to the *Sharee'ah*).

If the servant is responsible and accountable for everything: his hearing, his sight and his heart, it is therefore very becoming of him to call himself to account before the account is examined (ultimately, by Allaah). The obligation of calling oneself to account is established by His (تعالى) saying:

يَـٰٓأَيُّهَا ٱلَّذِينَ ءَامَنُوا۟ ٱتَّقُوا۟ ٱللَّهَ وَلْتَنظُرْ نَفْسٌ مَّا قَدَّمَتْ لِغَدٍ

> **O you who believe! Fear Allaah and keep your duty to Him. And let every person look to what he has sent forward for tomorrow...**[208]

The purport is that the rectification of the heart is achieved through calling one's self to account and its corruption is through negligence of one's soul and not restraining it.[209] Allaah is the One Who is sought for help and there is no power or might except by Allaah.

Ibn al-Qayyim, may Allaah have mercy upon him, said: "The soul invites to destructive matters, assists enemies, yearns every vulgarity and follows every evil. It, by its nature, adopts a course of violation.

---

[208] Soorah al-Hashr (59):18.

[209] Refer to *Ighaathah al-Lahfaan* of Ibn al-Qayyim, 1/97-100.

The blessing that is unequalled, is to come away from the soul and to be free of its yoke, for it is the greatest partition between the servant and Allaah (تعالى). The most knowledgeable people of the soul have the greatest contempt and abhorrence to it."[210]

We ask Allaah that he give us refuge from the evils of our souls and from the wickedness of our actions. Indeed, He is the most Munificent, the Generous.

2. External Causes

These are external causes or influences, which bear effect upon the eemaan by decreasing it. These are in reference to when the cause of the effect traces back to other then the person himself. Such causes can be generalised into three factors:

i. Shayt̲aan

He is held to be a strong external reason, which causes *eemaan* to decrease. *Shayt̲aan* is a vehement enemy to the believers. He awaits calamities to afflict them. He has no desire or goal other than to jolt the *eemaan* in the hearts of the believers and to weaken and corrupt it. Whoever submits to the whisperings of *Shayt̲aan*, complies with his notions and does not retreat to Allaah for refuge from him, his *eemaan* weakens and decreases. Indeed, it may disappear in its entirety depending on the Muslim's response to such whisperings and notions.

It is for this reason that Allaah has warned us of *Shayt̲aan* in the sternest sense and He has clarified his dangers, the detrimental consequences of following him as well as the fact that he is an enemy to the believers. Allaah ordered the believers to take him as an enemy and therefore deliver themselves from him and his whisperings.

---

[210] *Ighaathah al-Lahfaan*, 1/103.

Allaah (تعالى) says:

يَٰٓأَيُّهَا ٱلَّذِينَ ءَامَنُواْ لَا تَتَّبِعُواْ خُطُوَٰتِ ٱلشَّيْطَٰنِۚ وَمَن يَتَّبِعْ خُطُوَٰتِ ٱلشَّيْطَٰنِ فَإِنَّهُۥ يَأْمُرُ بِٱلْفَحْشَآءِ وَٱلْمُنكَرِۚ

"O you who believe! Do not follow the footsteps of *Shaytaan*, and whosoever follows the footsteps of *Shaytaan*, then, verily he (i.e., *Shaytaan*) commands *Fahshaa'* (i.e., to commit indecency and lewdness, etc.) and *al-Munkar* (i.e., disbelief, shirk, to do evil and wicked deeds, to speak or to do what is forbidden in Islaam, etc.)..."[211]

Allaah (تعالى) also says:

إِنَّ ٱلشَّيْطَٰنَ لَكُمْ عَدُوٌّ فَٱتَّخِذُوهُ عَدُوًّاۚ إِنَّمَا يَدْعُواْ حِزْبَهُۥ لِيَكُونُواْ مِنْ أَصْحَٰبِ ٱلسَّعِيرِ ﴿٦﴾

"Surely, *Shaytaan* is an enemy to you, so treat him as an enemy. He only invites his *hizb* (followers) that they may become the dwellers of the blazing Fire."[212]

Allaah (تعالى) says:

إِنَّ ٱلشَّيْطَٰنَ لِلْإِنسَٰنِ عَدُوٌّ مُّبِينٌ ﴿٥﴾

"Verily! *Shaytaan* is to man an open enemy!"[213]

Allaah (تعالى) also says:

ٱسْتَحْوَذَ عَلَيْهِمُ ٱلشَّيْطَٰنُ فَأَنسَىٰهُمْ ذِكْرَ ٱللَّهِۚ أُوْلَٰٓئِكَ حِزْبُ ٱلشَّيْطَٰنِۚ أَلَآ إِنَّ حِزْبَ ٱلشَّيْطَٰنِ هُمُ ٱلْخَٰسِرُونَ

"*Shaytaan* has taken hold of them. So he has made them forget the remembrance of Allaah. They are the party of *Shaytaan*. Verily, it is the party of *Shaytaan* that will be the losers!"[214]

---

[211] Soorah an-Noor (24):21.

[212] Soorah Faatir (35):6.

[213] Soorah Yoosuf (12):5.

[214] Soorah al-Mujaadilah (58):19

Ibn al-Jawzee says: "Hence it is an obligation upon the sane person to be on his guard against this enemy, who has manifested his enmity since the time of Aadam. He has sacrificed his life and self in corrupting the circumstances of the children of Aadam and Allaah has ordered one to be cautious of him..." He then mentioned a number of such texts and then said: "The like of this in the Qur'aan is abundant."[215]

Aboo Muhammad al-Maqdasee says in the introduction of his book *Dhamm al-Waswaas*: "To proceed, Allaah (سبحانه) has indeed made *Shaytaan* an enemy to man. He sits in wait against him along the straight path and comes to him from every direction and way, as Allaah (تعالى) has related from him that he said:

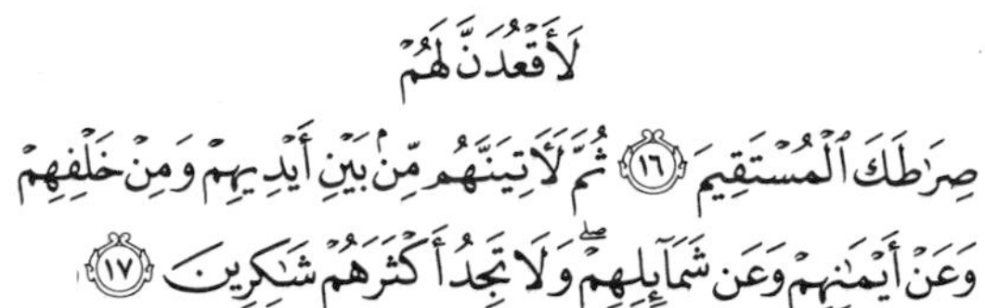

"Surely I will sit in wait against them on Your Straight Path. Then I will come to them from before them and behind them, from their right and from their left, and You will not find most of them as being grateful ones (i.e., they will not be dutiful to You)."[216]

Further, Allaah has warned us against following him and commanded us to possess animosity towards him and to oppose him, He (سبحانه) said:

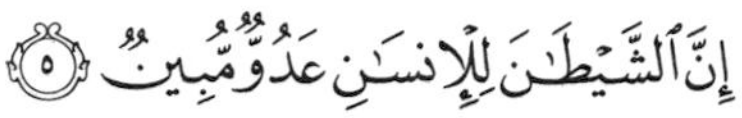

"Verily! *Shaytaan* is to man an open enemy!"[217]

[215] *Talbees Iblees*, pg. 23.

[216] Soorah al-A'raaf (7):16-17.

[217] Soorah Yoosuf (12):5.

He also said:

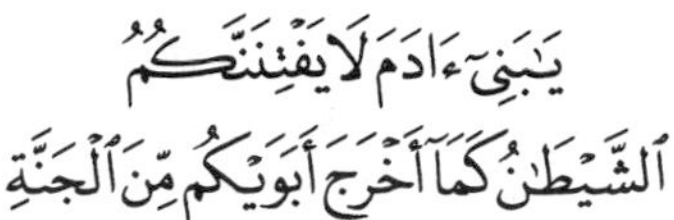

"O Children of Aadam! Do not let *Shaytaan* deceive you, as when he brought your parents (i.e., Aadam and Hawwaa') out of Paradise..."[218]

Allaah informed us of what he did with our parents as a way of cautioning us from obeying him and also to cut short any excuse for having followed him and Allaah (ﷻ) commanded us to follow the straight path..."[219]

Thus, *Shaytaan* is an enemy to man. His desire is to corrupt the beliefs and to wreak havoc on one's *eemaan*. Whoever does not fortify himself from him through remembrance of Allaah, resorting back to Allaah and seeking refuge with Him, will become a breeding ground for *Shaytaan*, who will lure him to actions of disobedience, entice him to perpetrate prohibited matters and push him to embark upon lewd sins. What a perish of his religion and what a corruption of his *eemaan* will it be if man submits to him!

Ibn al-Qayyim, may Allaah have mercy upon him, says: "Beware of enabling *Shaytaan* to establish himself in the very home of your thoughts and intentions, as he will corrupt them in such a manner that will make difficult its correction thereafter. He will cast all sorts of whisperings and harmful thoughts at you and he will prevent you from thinking about what may benefit you and it is you who have aided him against yourself by empowering him over your heart and thoughts and he then placed you in the possession of such thoughts."[*]

He, may Allaah have mercy upon him, put forward an excellent similitude in this regard, which lies in total agreement. He says in another excerpt from his book: "If you would like a consistent example for

---

[218] Soorah al-A'raaf (7):27.

[219] *Dhamm al-Waswaas*, pg.46. Also refer to Ibn al-Qayyim's introduction of his own book *Ighaathah al-Lahfaan*, 1/10.

[*] *Al-Fawaa'id*, pg. 309.

this, then his parable is that of a dog that is extremely famished; between you and the dog is a piece of meat or bread. He looks attentively at you and sees you not opposing him and he is so close to you. You drive him away and yell out at him and yet the dog refuses but to hover round you in circles and to try to deceive you with regard to what you possess in your hand."[220]

His intention, may Allaah have mercy upon him, behind this parable is to demonstrate the scope of *Shaytaan's* danger to man if he does not seek refuge with Allaah from him and fails to retreat back to Allaah for refuge from his evil, through beneficial words of supplication and blessed forms of remembrance.

However, whoever turns away and is instead averse to that, *Shaytaan* will cling to him in this way in which he will tempt and dictate to him until he eradicates his *eemaan*. Allaah (تعالى) says:

وَمَن يَعْشُ عَن ذِكْرِ ٱلرَّحْمَٰنِ نُقَيِّضْ لَهُۥ شَيْطَٰنًا
فَهُوَ لَهُۥ قَرِينٌ ﴿٣٦﴾ وَإِنَّهُمْ لَيَصُدُّونَهُمْ عَنِ ٱلسَّبِيلِ وَيَحْسَبُونَ
أَنَّهُم مُّهْتَدُونَ ﴿٣٧﴾ حَتَّىٰٓ إِذَا جَآءَنَا قَالَ يَٰلَيْتَ بَيْنِى وَبَيْنَكَ
بُعْدَ ٱلْمَشْرِقَيْنِ فَبِئْسَ ٱلْقَرِينُ ﴿٣٨﴾

> **"And whosoever turns away (blinds himself) from the remembrance of the Most Beneficent (i.e., this Qur'aan and worship of Allaah), We appoint for him a *shaytaan* to be a *Qareen* (i.e., an intimate companion) to him. And verily, they (i.e., *shaytaans*) hinder them from the Path (of Allaah), whilst they think that they are guided aright! Till, when (such a) one comes to Us, he says (to his *qareen*), 'Would that between me and you were the distance of the two Easts (or the East and West), a worst (type of) companion (you are indeed)!'"**[221]

---

[220] *At-Tibyaan fee Aqsaam al-Qur'aan*, pg. 419.

[221] Soorah az-Zukhruf (43):36-38.

ii. The World and its Allurements

This is the second external factor, which bears effect on a person's *eemaan* by decreasing it.

Hence, one of the causes of the decrease and weakness of *eemaan* is to be engrossed with the transient things of this temporary worldly life; to occupy one's time with it; be devoted to seeking it and to race after its pleasures, temptations and seductions.

Whenever the servants longing for this world intensifies and his heart becomes attached to it, his obedience will weaken and his *eemaan* will decrease accordingly. Ibn al-Qayyim, may Allaah have mercy upon him, says: "The extent of the servants desire for the world and of his pleasure with it determines his slackness towards obedience of Allaah and seeking the Hereafter."[222]

Accordingly, Allaah, the Wise, the All-Aware, censured the world in His Book and made clear its vileness and wretchedness in many *aayaat* in the Noble Qur'aan. Allaah (سبحانه) says:

ٱعْلَمُوٓا۟ أَنَّمَا ٱلْحَيَوٰةُ
ٱلدُّنْيَا لَعِبٌ وَلَهْوٌ وَزِينَةٌ وَتَفَاخُرٌۢ بَيْنَكُمْ وَتَكَاثُرٌ فِى ٱلْأَمْوَٰلِ
وَٱلْأَوْلَٰدِ ۖ كَمَثَلِ غَيْثٍ أَعْجَبَ ٱلْكُفَّارَ نَبَاتُهُۥ ثُمَّ يَهِيجُ فَتَرَىٰهُ
مُصْفَرًّا ثُمَّ يَكُونُ حُطَٰمًا ۖ وَفِى ٱلْءَاخِرَةِ عَذَابٌ شَدِيدٌ وَمَغْفِرَةٌ
مِّنَ ٱللَّهِ وَرِضْوَٰنٌ ۚ وَمَا ٱلْحَيَوٰةُ ٱلدُّنْيَآ إِلَّا مَتَٰعُ ٱلْغُرُورِ ﴿٢٠﴾

"Know that the life of this world is only play and amusement, pomp and mutual boasting among you, and rivalry in respect of wealth and children, just like the vegetation after rain, which pleases the tillers; afterwards it dries up and you see it turning yellow; then it becomes straw. But in the Hereafter there is a severe torment (for the disbe-

[222] *Al-Fawaa'id*, pg. 180.

lievers, evil-doers), and there is forgiveness from Allaah and (His) Good Pleasure (for the believers, good-doers), whereas the life of this world is only a deceiving enjoyment."[223]

Allaah (تعالى) also says:

وَٱضْرِبْ لَهُم مَّثَلَ ٱلْحَيَوٰةِ
ٱلدُّنْيَا كَمَآءٍ أَنزَلْنَٰهُ مِنَ ٱلسَّمَآءِ فَٱخْتَلَطَ بِهِۦ نَبَاتُ ٱلْأَرْضِ
فَأَصْبَحَ هَشِيمًا تَذْرُوهُ ٱلرِّيَٰحُ ۗ وَكَانَ ٱللَّهُ عَلَىٰ كُلِّ شَىْءٍ مُّقْتَدِرًا ﴿٤٥﴾
ٱلْمَالُ وَٱلْبَنُونَ زِينَةُ ٱلْحَيَوٰةِ ٱلدُّنْيَا ۖ وَٱلْبَٰقِيَٰتُ ٱلصَّٰلِحَٰتُ
خَيْرٌ عِندَ رَبِّكَ ثَوَابًا وَخَيْرٌ أَمَلًا ﴿٤٦﴾

"And put forward to them the example of the life of this world, it is like the water (rain), which We send down from the sky. The vegetation of the earth mingles with it, and becomes fresh and green. But (later) it becomes dry and broken pieces, which the winds then scatter. And Allaah is Able to do everything. Wealth and children are the adornment of the life of this world. But the everlasting righteous deeds are better with your Lord, for rewards and better in respect of hope."[224]

Allaah (تعالى) says:

وَفَرِحُوا۟ بِٱلْحَيَوٰةِ ٱلدُّنْيَا وَمَا ٱلْحَيَوٰةُ ٱلدُّنْيَا فِى ٱلْءَاخِرَةِ إِلَّا مَتَٰعٌ ﴿٢٦﴾

"...and they rejoice in the life of the world, whereas the life of this world as compared with the Hereafter is but a brief passing enjoyment."[225]

[223] Soorah al-Hadeed (57):20.

[224] Soorah al-Kahf (18):45-46.

[225] Soorah ar-Ra'd (13):26.

Allaah (تعالى) also says:

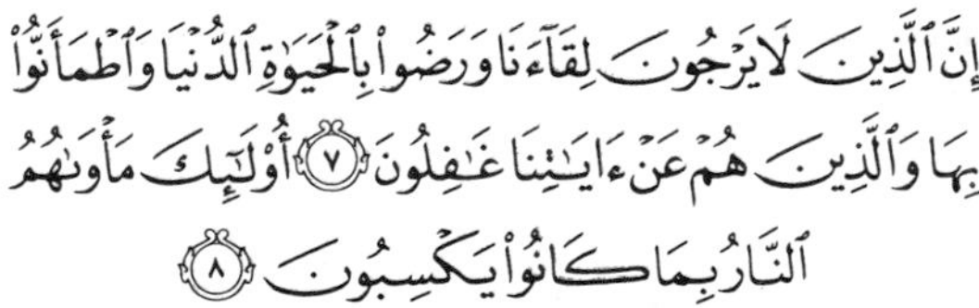

"Verily, those who hope not for their meeting with Us, but are pleased and satisfied with the life of the present world, and those who are heedless of Our *Aayaat* (proofs, evidences, verses, lessons, signs, revelations, etc.): Those, their abode will be the Fire, because of what they used to earn."[226]

This contains the greatest warning to one who is pleased with the life of this world, is comforted by it, is heedless of the *aayaat* of Allaah and who does not hope to meet Him.

Furthermore, Allaah says in censuring those of the believers who are pleased with this world:

يَٰٓأَيُّهَا ٱلَّذِينَ
ءَامَنُواْ مَا لَكُمْ إِذَا قِيلَ لَكُمُ ٱنفِرُواْ فِي سَبِيلِ ٱللَّهِ ٱثَّاقَلْتُمْ
إِلَى ٱلْأَرْضِۚ أَرَضِيتُم بِٱلْحَيَوٰةِ ٱلدُّنْيَا مِنَ ٱلْأٓخِرَةِۚ
فَمَا مَتَٰعُ ٱلْحَيَوٰةِ ٱلدُّنْيَا فِي ٱلْأٓخِرَةِ إِلَّا قَلِيلٌ ﴿٣٨﴾

"O you who believe! What is the matter with you, that when you are asked to march forth in the Cause of Allaah (i.e., *Jihaad*) you cling heavily to the earth? Are you pleased with the life of this world rather than the Hereafter? But little is the enjoyment of the life of this world as compared with the Hereafter."[227]

[226] Soorah Yoonus (10):7-8.

[227] Soorah at-Tawbah (9):38.

The Prophet (ﷺ) said: *"By Allaah, it is not poverty that I fear for you, but I fear that the world will be spread out for you just as it was spread out for those before you and then you will compete for it just as they competed for it and then you will be destroyed just as they were destroyed."* The *hadeeth* is agreed upon.[228] In another wording of theirs *"...you will be distracted just as they were distracted."*

There are other such texts, which are great in number. Thus, one who wants his *eemaan* to have growth, strength, safety from weakness and decrement must strive against his soul in distancing himself from this world, its temptations, seductions and distracting amusements, and what a multitude they are.

This can only be achieved and become true after considering two matters:

The first: to consider and look at the world, its rapid termination, passing away and disappearance; its deficiency and vileness; the pains of competing against one another for it and coveting it and what this contains of agony, embitterment and adversity.

The end of all that will be disappearance and discontinuance along with the regret and sorrow that follows on from it. Thus, its seeker can never be free of anxiety and worry before he attains it or even when he actually achieves it and he can never be free of grief and distress after it passes on.

The second: to consider and look at the Hereafter and its approach and arrival that is inevitable; its perpetuity and eternity; the glory of what it is within it of blessings and joy; the disparity between such things and what is in this world. It is as Allaah (سبحانه) said:

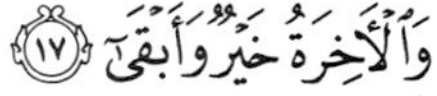

"Although the Hereafter is better and more lasting."[229]

---

[228] i.e., both al-Bukhaaree and Muslim relate it. [t] Al-Bukhaaree, (6/258, 7/320 *Fath*) and Muslim, 4/2273 from the *hadeeth* of 'Amr Ibn 'Awf, may Allaah be pleased with him.

[229] Soorah al-A'laa (87):17.

They are blessings that are perfect and everlasting, whereas these (things of the world) are fantasies that are deficient, sporadic and transitory.

If one contemplates over these two matters and considers them and looks into them in a proper manner, this will direct him to prefer the Everlasting Hereafter to the transient world.

The greatest aid for him in fulfilling this is to take a look at the state of Messenger (ﷺ) and his biography as well as his Companions. The fact that they renounced the world, turned their hearts away from it and discarded it. They never accustomed themselves with it and instead deserted it. They never inclined towards it and they regarded it to be a prison and not a heaven and thus, abstained from it in a true manner and if they had desired it they would have acquired every loved thing and arrived at every cherished matter from it. Indeed, the keys to the treasures of the world were offered to the Prophet but he rejected them. The world also poured out to the Companions but they did not opt for it and did not exchange their portion of the Hereafter for the world.

They knew that the world was a crossing point and passageway not a place of dwelling and settling, that it was a place of transit (*'uboor*) and not a place of happiness (*suroor*) and that it was a summer cloud which will soon disperse and an apparition no sooner is it completed than is it on the brink of departure.

As Allaah (تعالى) has said:

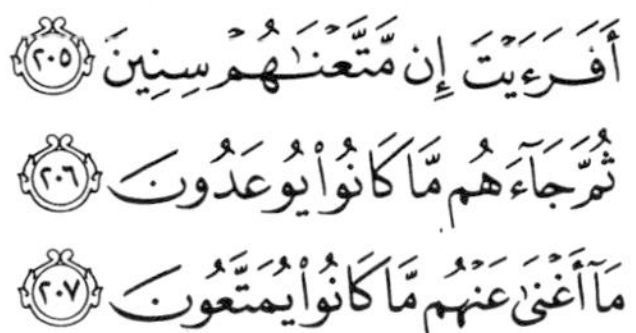

"Tell Me, if We do let them enjoy for a number of years, then afterwards comes to them that (punishment) which they had been promised; all that with which they used to enjoy shall not avail them."[230]

---

[230] Soorah ash-Shu'araa' (26):205-207.

He said:

وَيَوْمَ يَحْشُرُهُمْ كَأَن لَّمْ يَلْبَثُوٓاْ إِلَّا سَاعَةً مِّنَ ٱلنَّهَارِ يَتَعَارَفُونَ بَيْنَهُمْ

"And on the Day when He shall gather (resurrect) them together, (it will be as if) they had not stayed (in the life of this world and graves, etc.) but an hour of a day. They will recognise each other."[231]

He also said:

وَيَوْمَ تَقُومُ ٱلسَّاعَةُ يُقْسِمُ ٱلْمُجْرِمُونَ مَا لَبِثُواْ غَيْرَ سَاعَةٍ

"And on the Day that the Hour will be established, the *Mujrimoon* (criminals, disbelievers, polytheists, sinners, etc.) will swear that they stayed not but an hour..."[232]

Allaah is the one who is beseeched to aid us with *eemaan* and to protect us from trials and temptations, the apparent and hidden.

iii. Ill Associates

They are the most harmful people to a person's *eemaan*, behaviour and manners. Mixing with them and accompanying them is a great cause that decreases and weakens *eemaan*.

It has been established that the Prophet (ﷺ) said: *"A man is upon the deen (i.e., way of life) of his khaleel (i.e., close companion), so each one of you should look to see whom he takes as a khaleel."*[233]

Ibn 'Abdil-Barr said: "The meaning of this and Allaah knows best is that a person accustoms himself to the actions he views from those he accompanies and the (meaning of) *deen* is habitude. As such, he ordered one to only accompany the person who is seen to have (manners) that are graceful and beautiful, since goodness is mannerism.

---

[231] Soorah Yoonus (10):45.

[232] Soorah ar-Room (30):55.

[233] Related by Aboo Daawood, (13/179 *'Awn*); at-Tirmidhee, 4/589; Ahmad, 2/303; al-Haakim, 4/171 and al-Baghawee in *Sharh as-Sunnah*, 13/70 and it is a *hasan hadeeth*.

The saying of 'Adee Ibn Zayd embodies the meaning of this hadeeth:

About the person, do not question, but ask about his companion
Since every companion emulates the one he associates with

Likewise, the saying of Abee al-'Itaahiyyah:

Who could (still) remain unknown to you
If you were to look at his companion?

The like of this is very great. The meaning of this is that a person is not to associate with one who will lead him to actions and ways that are lamentable. As for the one who is not feared (to give such an effect) in this regard then there is no harm in accompanying him."[234]

Aboo Sulaymaan al-Khattaabee said: "His saying, 'A man is upon the *deen* (i.e., way of life) of his *khaleel* (i.e., close companion)' means: do not take as an intimate companion anyone other than one whose *deen* and trustworthiness you are pleased with, because when you do take one as an intimate companion, he will lead you to his *deen* and way. Do not endanger your *deen* or take a risk with your soul by taking as an intimate companion one whose *deen* and way is not pleasing.

Sufyaan Ibn 'Uyaynah said: "It has been transmitted in connection to this *hadeeth*, 'Look at Fir'awn, with him was Haamaan. Look at al-Hajjaaj, with him was Yazeed Ibn Abee Muslim, who was worse than he was. Look at Sulaymaan Ibn 'Abdul-Malik; he was accompanied by Rajaa' Ibn Haywah, who then put him aright and directed him.'

It is said that *al-Khullah* is derived from 'The love interpenetrated (*takhallala*) the heart and firmly established itself within it'. It is the highest level of brotherhood and that is because people are initially strangers to each other. Once they attain a familiarity, they strike harmony with each other, so they become good friends. If they become homogeneous, they then have love for each other and if this love intensifies it becomes *khullah*."[235]

---

[234] *Bahjah al-Majaalis*, 2/751.

[235] *Al-'Uzlah*, pg. 56.

It has also been said, 'People are like flocks of sand grouse[236]' because of the resemblance of form they bear to each other and also because of their imitation of the actions of each other. It is for this reason that the one who initiates good or evil will carry the same share of reward or sin of the one who follows him.[237]

Some wise folk have said: "The pillar of love is homogeneity and every love or friendship that is not based on homogeneity is swift to dwindle and be over."[238]

The reason for the prohibition on mixing with associates of evil and for the warning of taking company with them is that the make up of a person is naturally disposed for emulating and copying whoever he associates with. Thus, taking company with students of knowledge stirs in oneself the eager desire to seek knowledge. Taking company with ascetics, causes one to renounce worldly pleasures. Taking company with the people of desires causes one to tumble into the abysses of innovations and taking company with one who covets the world stirs in oneself the eager desire for the world and so on.

As such, it is essential that a person chooses of his colleagues and associates those who will be bring about for him good and benefit because of mixing with them.

One who reflects on the condition of the *Salaf* and contemplates on their life histories will come to know this and he will observe their severe caution and warning against associates of evil be them *fussaaq*, innovators or others.[239]

Aboo Dardaa' said: "It is from the intelligence of the servant (to consider and be aware) of whom he walks with, enters with and exits

---

[236] i.e., a type of game-bird. [t]

[237] Refer to *al-Istiqaamah* by Ibn Taymiyyah, 2/255.

[238] *Al-'Uzlah* by al-Khattaabee, pg. 62.

[239] Look up on this for example, *al-'Uzlah* by al-Khattaabee, pg. 56 and onwards, *al-Ibaanah* of Ibn Battah, 2/431 and onwards and others.

with." Aboo Qilaabah, who related this account, then said: "May Allaah fight[240] the poet who said:

About the person, do not question, but look at his companion
Since the companion emulates the one he associates with[241]

Al-Asma'ee said concerning this verse of poetry: "*I have not seen a verse more similar to the Sunnah than this one*"[242]

It has also been reported on 'Abdullaah Ibn Mas'ood that he said: "Assess people by their intimates, for a person only befriends one whom appeals to him and whom he admires."

Al-A'mash also relates: "They (i.e., the *Salaf*) did not ask about a person after (having ascertained) three (things): whom he used to walk with, whom he used to enter with and whom his acquaintances were among the people."

Sufyaan said: "There is nothing more influential upon the corruption or rectification of an individual than a companion."

Qataadah said: "Indeed, By Allaah, we have not witnessed a person accompany except one who is like him and of his own manner, so accompany the righteous from the slaves of Allaah, you may then be with them or like them"

Al-Fudayl said: "It is not for the believer to sit with anyone he desires…"[243]

Narratives of this sort are numerous, the mention of which would be lengthy. I have however, selected from them a subsistent and adequate amount. One who ponders over these cited accounts as well as oth-

---

[240] Not to be taken in its literal sense in this context, since the Arabs employ such terms in different ways and at times they use phrases containing words of censure but actually intend meanings of the opposite such as praise and amazement. [t]

[241] Related by al-Khattaabee in *al-'Uzlah*, pg. 59 and Ibn Battah in *al-Ibaanah*, 2/439.

[242] *Al-Ibaanah* of Ibn Battah, 2/440.

[243] These accounts have been related by Ibn Battah in *al-Ibaanah*, (2/439, 452, 476, 480 & 481).

ers, will know of the danger there is to the individual's religion and character in associating with people of evil, *fisq* and *fujoor*.

You may witness a person who is upright, virtuous and righteous, when he mingles and associates with people of evil and *fisq* and accompanies them, he becomes a *faasiq* and *faajir* like them and this is the pattern of Allaah in his creation.

Hence, mixing with the *fussaaq* and people of evil is one of the most severe causes for the decrease and weakness of *eemaan*. In fact, even for its disappearance and annihilation and that is dependent upon the condition of evil of such people as well as the level of mingling with them.

Conclusion

This is a blessed section from the causes behind the increase and decrease of *eemaan*, which I have compiled for you - my noble brother - from assorted places and diverse sources, as an insight and forewarning for you.

It is Allaah, al-Kareem, Who I ask of *tawfeeq* and correctness for you and myself. The end of our supplication is that All praise is for Allaah, the Lord of the Worlds and may He exalt, send peace, blessings and favour His servant and Messenger, our Prophet Muhammad, his family and all of his Companions.

Glossary

Aayaat: see *aayah*.

Aayah: (pl. *aayaat*) Sign; miracle; example, lesson... The *aayaat* of Allaah are of two types:
(1) The *aayaat* that are heard, i.e., the verses of the Qur'aan.
(2) The *aayaat* that are observed/witnessed, i.e., Allaah's creation of the sun, moon, stars, rivers, mountains, etc.

Ahl al-Kitaab: People of the book; jews and christians.

Ahl as-Sunnah wa al-Jamaa'ah: The body or people of *Sunnah*, who follow the way of the Prophet as opposed to innovations and the people of *Jamaa'ah*, who remain united to the truth and preserve the original unity and way of the early generation of Muslims as opposed to those who have split and deviated from this way.

Amaanaat: Plural of *amaanah*. All the duties ordained by Allaah including covenants between the person and his Lord as well as that between him and his fellow men.

Awliyaa': One who offers or is offered *walaa'* (Amity; allegiance; loyalty. *Walaa'* combines three principal matters: to assist, love and be in agreement.) Allaah describes two main features of his *walee* in the Qur'aan as one who has *eemaan* and *taqwaa*.

Deenar: Dinar, a currency.

Dirham: Pence; money; a currency.

Eemaan: See Translator's Introduction.

Faajir: Doer of *fujoor*.

Faasiq: (pl. Fusaaq) Doer of *fisq*.

Faqeeh: Jurist; one who is learned in *fiqh*; one of sound understanding.

Fawaahish: Lewd and reprehensible sins; illegal sexual relations.

Firdaws: The highest level of *Jannah*.

Fisq: (pl. *fusooq*) Immorality, transgression, wickedness, etc.

Fitan: Plural of *fitnah*; trials, tribulations and temptations.

Fujoor: Wickedness, sins, evil-doing, etc.

Fusaaq: see *faasiq*.

Fusooq: see *fisq*.

Hadeeth: A narration composed of the utterances of the Prophet, his actions, character, physical description or tacit approval.

Hajj: One of the pillars of Islaam, the pilgrimage to Makkah.

Inaabah: To turn to Allaah in repentance.

Kalaam: Speech, discourse; dialectics: scholastic theology.

Kalaamiyyah: Pertaining to *kalaam*.

Khateeb: One who delivers a sermon, especially for Friday prayer.

Kufr: Rejection of *eemaan*; disbelief; covering up of the truth and rejection of Allaah, His Messengers and Religion.

Riyaa': An act of worship undertaken by someone to be seen and praised by others and not purely for Allaah.

Sadaqah: Alms, charity; obligatory or recommended type.

Saheehayn: The 'two *Saheehs*' i.e., *Saheeh al-Bukhaaree* and *Saheeh Muslim*.

Salaf: Predecessors; more often employed to mean the Righteous Predecessors consisting of the Companions and the next two generations after them.

Sharee'ah: Divine Islamic law as ordained by Allaah.

Shaytaan: (pl. *shayaateen*) a devil; The devil, Iblees.

Soorah: (plural: *suwar*) A chapter of the Noble Qur'aan.

Ta'teel: In the context of Allaah's names and attributes, to negate them or the meanings they entail.

Taabi'een: Plural of *taabi'ee*: A follower; a student and follower of the companions in righteousness.

Tahleel: To say *laa Ilaaha Illa Allaah*.

Tahreef: In the context of Allaah's names and attributes, to misconstrue the wording or the meaning of the particular term.

Takbeer: In the context of the book: to say *Allaah Akbar*.

Takyeef: In the context of Allaah's names and attributes, to either specify or question the actual qualitative designation of an attribute.

Targheeb: Arouse interest, awake desire; to mention matters that cause one to desire to do good, seek the reward of such actions and strive to attain Paradise, etc.

Tarheeb: Frightening; to mention matters that cause one to abandon the perpetration of bad deeds and fear their consequences and the Fire, etc.

Tasbeeh: In the context of the book: to say *subhaan Allaah* or use other words in praising and glorifying Allaah.

Tawakkul: Reliance; Reliance upon Allaah through both entrusting affairs to Him as well as adopting the causes that Allaah has measured out.

Tawfeeq: In the context of this book, the success conferred to the slave by Allaah.

Tawheed: To single out Allaah in areas exclusive to Him: Lordship, His names and attributes and worship.

Zakaah: One of the pillars of the religion, the tax levied on a Muslim's wealth that meets certain criteria.

Zuhaad: Plural of *zaahid*: one who practises *zuhd*.

Zuhd: Asceticism.